T5-CCW-255

Hands-On Science

Ruth M. Young, M.S.Ed.

Teacher Created Materials, Inc.

Cover Design by Darlene Spivak

Copyright © 1995 Teacher Created Materials, Inc. All rights reserved.

No part of this publication may be reproduced in whole or in part, or stored in any retrieval system, or transmitted in any form or by any means, electronic, mechanical, photocopying, recording, or otherwise, without written permission from the publisher, Teacher Created Materials, Inc., 6421 Industry Way, Westminster, CA 92683.

Made in U.S.A.
ISBN 1-55734-841-3
Order Number TCM 841

Table of Contents

Introduction

Science in the elementary school is all too frequently considered a subject which is less important than all the others. If it is taught at all, it is usually done through *reading* about science rather than *doing* science. This needs to be corrected, since the study of our natural world is of vital importance and interest to all students. Teachers who breathe life into the study of science will forever be fondly remembered by their students.

After thirty years of teaching, 16 as an elementary science teacher, the author of this book has set a goal to inspire elementary teachers to actively involve their students in the excitement of studying science. This book is designed to share teaching techniques, ideas for activities, resources, and other information gleaned and tested with K–6 grade students over these many years. Hopefully, it will empower the teachers who read this book with the incentive and ability to go forth and develop great science programs for their students.

Overview

What is science?

Natural phenomena occurs on Earth and throughout the universe. Science is the body of knowledge which has been formed by countless human minds observing and experimenting to describe and explain the mysteries of natural phenomena. Science is learned by investigating and experiencing the natural world around us.

Science is learned by investigating and experiencing the natural world around us.

Why teach activity oriented science?

Did you learn to drive by reading a book, then getting behind the wheel and heading for the open road? Does a child learn to walk by watching a film or videotape? What science process skills are being used when working at the computer? Can students learn science from reading a book, listening to a teacher, viewing films or videos, or doing lessons on the computer if these are based on science facts? The answer to these questions is absolutely NO. Wait, you may be saying, didn't you just state that science is a body of knowledge? It is true that there is a body of scientific knowledge, but teaching students science facts is not as important as developing their science process skills so they can learn this knowledge on their own.

Science is not simply a collection of facts; it is a discipline of thinking about rational solutions to problems after establishing the basic facts derived from observations. It is hypothesizing from what is known to what might be, and then attempting to test the hypotheses. The love for logical thinking must come first; the facts can later fall into place. Rosalyn S. Yalow, Nobel Laureate (Medicine 1977) speaking at commencement, 1988, Drew University.

"The present science textbooks and methods of instruction, far from helping, often actually impede progress toward science literacy. They emphasize the learning of answers more than the exploration of questions, memory at the expense of critical thought, bits and pieces of information instead of understandings in context, recitation over argument, reading in lieu of doing. They fail to encourage students to work together, to share ideas and information freely with each other, or to use modern instruments to extend their intellectual capabilities" (American Association for the Advancement of Science, 1990, p. XVI).

It is the role of elementary teachers to impart the excitement and joy of learning science to their students.

Should I teach the scientific method?

The scientific method is a myth which is frequently misused in elementary science textbooks and classrooms to standardize the teaching of science. Indeed, scientists do not use any step-by-step scientific method when conducting experiments. The step-by-step process dictated by the scientific method is of no value in the elementary classroom, rather it is important to place emphasis on students doing science. By being physically involved in the study of science, students will develop the process skills which are so vital, as well as reach an understanding of the science content.

"There are no preordained conclusions in science. However, along with the legendary open-endedness and serendipity of science goes another very important factor. Scientists build expectation of what will happen on a tremendous pre-existing body of observations, facts, inferences, hypotheses, and theories. They use the expectations to guide further inquiry" (California State Department of Education 1990, p.15).

It is the role of elementary teachers to impart the excitement and joy of learning science to their students. The goal should be to teach conceptual understanding of factual knowledge through application of the "science process skills." Teaching science through the use of the scientific method will never achieve that goal.

What are the science process skills?

The science process skills students should use when conducting hands-on science experiments are:

- ◆ *Observing*—gathering information through the senses of smelling, tasting, touching, looking, and hearing
- ◆ *Communicating*—exchanging and discussing ideas
- ◆ *Comparing*—looking at similarities and differences
- ◆ *Ordering*—placing objects or phenomena along a continuum, sequencing events logically or in a cycle
- ◆ *Categorizing*—grouping objects or events together by like characteristics
- ◆ *Relating*—recognizing relationships between and among events which involve interactions, dependencies, and cause-and-effect
- ◆ *Inferring*—forming answers from logical reasoning based upon observed evidence
- ◆ *Applying*—putting knowledge to work to create or understand an idea, phenomenon, or object, to solve a problem

The skill of categorizing is useful in the study of many science topics such as minerals, insects, and birds.

How are the science process skills taught?

The list of science process skills is a hierarchy which should serve as a guide to developing science activities that begin at lower levels, such as observation and communicating, and gradually progress to higher levels, such as relating and inferring. Even primary students should be given the opportunity to use the higher level skills when appropriate.

The skill of categorizing is useful in the study of many science topics such as minerals, insects, and birds. An activity to demonstrate how to sort by various properties could use the students' shoes, as shown in "The Sorting Game," an excerpt from *Rocks and Minerals* (Young, 1994) found on page 6. As the students sort their shoes by a variety of characteristics they are developing their ability to observe, communicate, compare, and categorize.

Collecting data is another skill which relates to those listed earlier. An example of this relationship is demonstrated in the activity "Blow It Up" from *Easy Chemistry* (Barry, 1994) found on page 7. Students conduct an experiment with vinegar and baking soda in a bottle with a balloon over the mouth of the bottle. They collect data about the circumference of the balloon before and after baking soda is added to the vinegar. The skills of observing, comparing, relating, and inferring are being practiced in this lesson. As an extender of this lesson, the amounts of vinegar and baking soda are varied and data on the size of the balloon is recorded. This further develops students' science process skills.

Science process skills can only be taught through experiencing science. These skills are not developed by reading, listening to lectures, watching demonstrations, videos, or movies, or working on a computer. Consider the difference between connecting a real battery to a light bulb and getting it to light as opposed to simulating this on a computer. By manipulating the materials students use their skills of observing, relating, inferring, and applying. These skills are not being honed when the activity is done via computer simulation. The thrill of science can only be fully realized through direct involvement. It is necessary to engage students in science activities by placing them in a position of responsibility for the learning task. Students should be provided with experimental problem-solving experiences where the result has direct meaning for them (California State Department of Education, 1990). Science activities should be carefully designed to teach science concepts through activities, as shown in the physical education curriculum connection from *Space* (Young, 1994) shown on page 8.

Should you become interested in using science computer programs, use the criteria for selecting science teacher guides outlined in the "Getting Started" chapter on page 10. Select computer programs which are not just an electronic textbook, unless they will be used to provide background knowledge for students. Try to find programs which require the students to do some hands-on activities in order to complete the computer lesson. Science knowledge is needed to serve as background for lessons but should not take all the science time; most of this should be spent on activities which develop an understanding of science concepts and improve the science skills. More details on lessons and units are found in the "Getting Started" and "Designing a Science Unit" chapters.

What is the purpose of this book?

It is the goal of the author to enable all teachers who read this book to have the resources, knowledge, and enthusiasm to develop meaningful, hands-on science programs for their students. This book is designed for experienced as well as new teachers. The hints and ideas you read herein have been tested over years with elementary students who had a variety of ability levels, ethnic backgrounds, and languages. Letting students DO science is the key to making it exciting and worthwhile, as long as the activities are carefully written.

Letting students DO science is the key to making it exciting and worthwhile, as long as the activities are carefully written.

Do not be intimidated by a lack of science knowledge; you can learn along with the students and from them. Remember, learning continues throughout our lives. It is important for students to realize that even their teacher does not know everything, but is anxious to improve his or her skills and knowledge. This sets a wonderful model for the children in your classroom.

Hopefully, as you read the chapters which follow, you will begin to develop a growing feeling of confidence and eagerness to teach science often and continuously throughout the school year. Your students will benefit from your enthusiasm to teach hands-on science. They already possess a natural curiosity about scientific phenomenon and only need to be taught techniques for learning how to understand it.

The next chapter, "Getting Started," will provide you with ideas that should assist you in developing exciting and meaningful science lessons.

The Sorting Game

Question

How can things be sorted?

Setting the Stage

- Tell students you are going to sort them into groups and that you want them to see if they can guess how you are sorting them.
- Sort students into two groups by sex, without letting the students know your system. Do this by calling on students one at a time to go to a specific area of the room so they will join the boys' or girls' group.
- After you have selected five or six students, see if the students can guess your system of sorting by asking a few students to join the group to which they think they belong.
- Explain to students that there are a variety of ways to sort things and that they will do an activity to demonstrate this.

Materials Needed for Each Individual

- one of their shoes
- data capture sheet
  Note to the teacher: The students will use their shoes to learn how to sort them according to various properties.

Procedure

1. Seat students in a large circle on the floor and ask them to remove one shoe. (You should also add one of your shoes.)
2. Place the shoes side by side and ask students to suggest a way they can be sorted using only one property at a time (e.g., color, fabric, size).
3. Have two students sort the shoes into piles according to the property chosen by the class.
4. Now have students choose another property by which to sort the shoes.
5. Have students record on their data capture sheets the different properties by which the shoes were sorted. Then, mark the number of shoes that possessed each property.

Extensions

Have students continue this activity until they know that they can use one property at a time for sorting the shoes, but that there are many different properties from which to choose.

Closure

Divide students into groups of three or four and give each group a deck of cards from which the jokers have been removed. Tell students to sort the cards. Have them repeat the sorting using other properties. Discuss the variety of properties used by each group to do the sorting.

Reprinted from TCM636 Rocks and Minerals Primary, *Teacher Created Materials, 1994*

Blow It Up

In the space provided below, record the data and answer the questions.

Event	Describe what happened to the balloon.	Circumference of Blown Balloon (cm)	Did a chemical change occur? Why?
Ballon & Vinegar			
Balloon, Baking Soda, & Vinegar			

Reprinted from TCM648 Easy Chemistry Intermediate *Teacher Created Materials, 1994*

Physical Education

Let students experience how difficult it is to launch and land a vehicle on the moon by experiencing a simulation of this task.

Science Concept: The moon travels around the Earth approximately every 28 days. The Earth spins on its axis once every 24 hours and travels around the sun in 365 1/4 days.

Note to the teacher:

The teacher will need to sketch two concentric circles on the playground. One circle should be a diameter of 3' (1 m) inside of a circle 10' (3 m) in diameter.

This lesson can also be conducted on a simple children's merry-go-round often found at a neighborhood park.

- Have your class assemble around the large circle, leaving about 5' (1.5 m) of space between them and the edge of the circle.
- Select two students, one to represent the Earth and the other the moon.
- Have *Earth* stand on the edge of the inside circle and *Moon* on the outside circle.
- They should toss a tennis ball back and forth to practice catching it while standing still.
- Once students become adept at catching the ball, have *Earth* begin to move around its circle in a counterclockwise direction, continuing to toss and catch the ball.
- Now, simulate the launch and landing of a lunar vehicle by having *Moon* walk slowly around the larger circle in the same direction as *Earth*. Continue tossing the *Lunar Transporter* between *Earth* and *Moon*.
- This simulates a real life dilemma of launching a space vehicle from the moving Earth and landing it on the moon, which is moving around the Earth during the three days required to make the trip.

Reprinted from TCM639 Space Intermediate, *Teacher Created Materials, 1994*

Getting Started

What science topics should I teach?

If you have the freedom to select your own science topics rather than teach those specified by the school district, choose topics which are of direct interest to your students and you. Earthquakes would be appropriate to study in most of California but would be of little interest in Idaho. The main purpose is not to teach scientific facts but to provide direct experiences in science through hands-on activities which are meaningful and develop conceptual understanding. If students are learning about the area in which they live, it has far more meaning to them. It is also more important to cover a few science topics in depth, rather than doing a shallow study of many.

> **It is also more important to cover a few science topics in depth, rather than doing a shallow study of many.**

Find a science topic which excites you, and the students will be excited by your lessons. Since you want to teach science through activities, avoid topics which are too sophisticated or theoretical for the children. Time spent teaching about quasars in the elementary grades is not as valuable as studying the phases of the moon. An example lesson on the phases of the moon is included on pages 18 and 19.

Your students can be involved in activities which help them understand the phases of the moon but will not be able to comprehend what a quasar is. They can apply their knowledge of the moon by observing and recording it throughout the month, thus adding to their science knowledge, as well as improving their skills.

The topics you choose to teach should be a balance of earth, life, and physical sciences. These include the topics shown below:

◆ Earth: astronomy, geology, oceanography, and meteorology
◆ Life: living things, cells, genetics, evolution, and ecosystems
◆ Physical: matter, chemical reactions, force, and energy

There are a wide variety of hands-on science guides available for elementary teachers.

When possible, lessons should illustrate that these sciences are interrelated rather than distinctly different. Examples of this include an activity to show that tides are caused by the moon, which combines the studies of oceanography and astronomy. A study of climate changes influencing the evolution of life integrates meteorology and evolution. Grouping science units during the year so that they flow from one science area to the next helps students see these relationships.

Where can I find ideas for science topics?

There are a wide variety of hands-on science guides available for elementary teachers. These may be purchased at major bookstores, teacher supply stores, science conferences, and through catalogs. The annotated "Resource" section of this book lists a sample of these. Use the following criteria when selecting any of these guides:

◆ Does the author have the science background needed to write about the topic?

◆ Are there many quality activities found throughout the guide?

◆ Are the activities in a sequential order leading to higher levels of thinking?

◆ Are the activities clearly explained and appropriate for your students?

◆ Do the activities use materials that are easy to obtain?

◆ Is there authentic assessment related to the activities or can you develop it yourself from the ideas in the guide?

◆ Is accurate science background information provided?

◆ Does the guide list additional resources?

You can find topics for your students to study by looking at the area around your school or local science museums. If there is a pond, lake, stream, or other water source, a study of microbiology or other water life is appropriate. A wooded area opens up a wealth of opportunities for the study of plants, birds, mammals, and the entire ecology of that area.

Natural history museums often have displays which are related to the local area. They may also offer curriculum materials which are activities to be done before visiting the museum to prepare students so they are able to apply what they have learned. Sometimes this will involve the students in gathering data from the displays through observations, then analyzing it after they return to school. This provides better opportunities for learning from the study trip experience. If there are no curriculum materials available, the teacher should preview the displays and design them for his or her class. This will make the study trip meaningful, rather than just a casual visit to the museum.

You can find topics for your students to study by looking at the area around your school or local science museums.

Avoid spending time on topics which are unrelated to your students' everyday experiences. An example of this is the study of a tropical rain forest. Students will develop only a superficial appreciation for a rain forest by looking at pictures or films. Unless they live in a location where they can personally experience a rain forest, it is better to spend time studying the interaction between the plants and animals in their own area. The goal is to help the students understand why there is a need to safeguard any ecosystem. Once they have learned to examine this relationship, they will have developed skills which can be applied to appreciating ecosystems found in any area.

Membership in the local, state, and national science organizations will offer ideas for science topics. These associations frequently have newsletters or journals which are sent to members. Science curriculum ideas which have been developed by teachers are included in these periodicals. Perhaps the best known of these science organizations is the National Science Teachers Association which supplies members with a wealth of information through four journals, the *NSTA Reports* newsletter, and an annual extensive list of science suppliers. The "Resources" section of this book has further details regarding science materials and organizations of interest to teachers.

What are the elements of a good science lesson?

Good science lessons should be "user friendly" and appeal to you and your students. Each lesson should be activity oriented and cover only one science concept or big idea. Lessons linked together in a logical sequence form a unit of study about a science topic. These statements apply to activities found in commercial teacher guides or those you design. The description of an activity should contain most of the elements shown below. The activity may not use these exact titles, but most of the information should be found in the text of the activity.

- ◆ *Title:* Tells the topic of the activity at a glance.
- ◆ *Objective:* Tells what students should learn from this activity.
- ◆ *Grade Level:* Designates the grade level(s) for which the activity is most appropriate.
- ◆ *Background Information:* Provides science concepts (facts) for the students and/or teacher.
- ◆ *Materials:* Gives a complete list of the materials needed to conduct the activity.
- ◆ *Preparation:* Describes what materials the teacher needs to prepare or collect prior to teaching the activity.
- ◆ *Motivator:* Gives ideas for an introduction to the activity which focus the students' attention on the topic to be covered.
- ◆ *Activity (Procedure):* Provides an outline of how to conduct the activity.
- ◆ *Closure:* Suggests a way of ending the activity and assuring it has been meaningful to the students.
- ◆ *Extender:* Gives suggestions for continuing the activity, perhaps by integrating other subject areas where appropriate.
- ◆ *Assessment:* Describes methods to assess the students' learning from the activity.

Motivators are used at the beginning of a lesson to focus the students' attention on the activity which they will be doing.

Ideas for Motivators

Motivators are used at the beginning of a lesson to focus the students' attention on the activity which they will be doing. The motivator should get all students' attention. Some methods of motivating students are described below and on the following page.

Question: Ask the students a question which relates to the lesson which you are about to teach. Give them time to think of their answers, then have them share these with a group of one or two other students.

Example: When initiating an activity on earthquake legends you could say, "Have you ever felt an earthquake? Think of this experience and be ready to tell the students in your group where you were, how it felt, and how you reacted to it."

Ideas for Demonstration
Do a demonstration which may be something unusual or unexpected. This can be referred to as the jaw-dropper method.

Example: When introducing an activity using indicator dyes, do a magic show. Boil a quarter head of red cabbage in water until the water turns dark blue. Drain off the blue water and fill three small test tubes or jars. Place drops of ammonia (base) in one container of "cabbage juice" and it will turn green. Add drops of clear vinegar (acid) to another container and it becomes violet. Keep the third as a control to compare the color changes of the other two. Do not let the students know what chemicals you have used, but let them discover it as they experiment with cabbage juice and a variety of acids and bases to see and record the reactions.

Review Previous Lesson
Remind students of an earlier activity which directly relates to the one they are about to do (see "Setting the Stage" from Broken Egg and Cracked Earth at the end of this chapter on pages 20 and 21). This strengthens their understanding of the concepts covered in that lesson and also helps them see the link to the new activity. The activity they do in this lesson may even be a continuation of the last lesson, so carry-over data will be used.

Ideas for Bulletin Board Displays
Display science pictures which relate to the science topic. Describe them to the students, then allow time for them to look at the pictures for a few minutes before the lesson begins. Calendars and posters are a wonderful source for spectacular science photographs on a wide range of topics. Bulletin boards may also be interactive. One way to do this is to use them as a place to record data, such as the daily high and low temperatures which will be graphed and analyzed by the students.

Create a Science Table
A display of various seeds, mounted insects, magnetic pendulum, mineral specimens, or other science items of interest can grab the students' attention and awaken their curiosity. This can lead into activities to investigate the items further. Unusual materials for this center can be found in nature or purchased at science museum shops or science stores, such as The Nature Company. If the teacher initiates a What Is It? table where "science stuff" is displayed, students will bring oddities which they want to display. As they search for unusual science stuff, the students develop a greater awareness of nature, which is what you want to happen.

Calendars and posters are a wonderful source for spectacular science photographs on a wide range of topics.

13

What is a science activity?

Many activities labeled as science by some authors and teachers illustrate that they do not understand how science differs from other subjects. What follows are examples of activities mislabeled as science compared to actual science activities.

Unit Topic: Astronomy

> Activity: Writing biographical sketches of astronomers. This is a social studies and language arts activity, not science.

> Science: Reproducing the discoveries made by Galileo, an early astronomer. Galileo Galilei, in 1609, was the first person to observe the moon through a telescope. He saw that it was not smooth, as most people thought, but had craters. He also looked at Jupiter and saw four moons near it. Night after night, he observed and recorded their locations. He soon discovered that the moons were not orbiting Earth but revolved around Jupiter! This broke all the astronomical rules of his day, since it was firmly believed that all astronomical objects—sun, planets, and stars,—revolved around the Earth.

> Students can use binoculars to see what Galileo discovered about the moon and compare it with the view they see with the naked eye. They can also use binoculars to observe Jupiter at night and observe and record the locations of the moons over several weeks. Now, the study has become earth science.

Unit Topic: Dinosaurs

> Activity: Students trace the outlines of dinosaurs, cut them out, and paste them on a page on which they write facts about the dinosaurs. This lesson is language arts, not science.

> Science: A comparison of dinosaur skeletons with bones from a variety of present-day animals, including those of humans, will change this into a life science activity.

Unit Topic: Pulleys

> Activity: Students look at drawings of a variety of pulleys and read how they lift heavy objects. They fill in a worksheet which asks questions that can be answered by reading the text. This is reading for comprehension, which is language arts, not science.

Many activities labeled as science by some authors and teachers illustrate that they do not understand how science differs from other subjects.

Science: A variety of pulleys are placed around the room for students to try to lift an object and discover which pulley system makes the job easiest. They draw the pulley system, lift the mass, and use a spring balance to determine the effort required to lift the mass. The information is recorded under their drawing. This is repeated with each different pulley and compared at the end of the tests to find the best pulley system to use. Now, the lesson becomes a physical science activity.

Science activities need to center around studies of earth, life, or physical science, not social studies, art, or language arts. There are many unit topics that will use two or three areas of science. Evolution is an example of this since it includes changes in the geological features of Earth (earth science), plant and animal life (life science), and gases of the atmosphere (physical science).

Closure Techniques
There are many techniques for closing an activity to summarize what students have learned and enhance their understanding. These include:

Science Journals
Students may keep science journals for each of the topics they study during the year. Journal entries may include data which is gathered during an activity, drawings to illustrate a concept, or a story to describe something they learned. Science journals may form the basis of a student's portfolio. (See the "Designing a Unit" chapter for further information about portfolios.)

Funwork
Funwork is a form of homework which is an assignment to be accomplished outside of class. This may involve research the students will do such as conducting a survey by interviewing friends and family. It may be drawings of the moon's phases each night for several weeks. Students may be issued an inexpensive magnet to take home and make a list of items to which the magnet would and would not stick. The assignment may be to teach the concept learned in the activity to members of the family. See "Extensions" in the Broken Egg lesson on page 20 for additional extender ideas.

Sharing Information
If the activity involved gathering data, the students should share the results with the class. This may be done by having them work in groups to gather their data with each group having a

Science activities need to center around studies of earth, life, or physical science, not social studies, art, or language arts.

15

recorder to write the data on the board so all data can be compared. For instance, if students are collecting weather data, several groups could be assigned to collect the same data such as temperatures in various locations, type and amount of clouds, humidity, and barometric pressure. When the information has been recorded by each group, it is compared to find any errors, then averaged to create that day's weather report.

Ideas for Extenders
Other subject areas may be used to extend the lessons but should enhance the learning of the science concept. Some examples are described below:

Language Arts
There are outstanding books which fit many science topics. Reading aloud the story *Maia, A Dinosaur Grows Up*, (Horner and Gorman, 1989) would be a good way to extend a study of dinosaurs through the use of literature. This method could also serve as a motivator for the lesson.

Science concepts learned in an activity can also be shared with others outside the class. This can be done through the publication of a science newsletter, writing and performing a play, or presenting a science lesson for another classroom.

Mathematics
Mathematics and science are often interrelated. A study of other planets can be enhanced by having students determine their weights on different planets.

Graphing data on the frequency of various lengths of pendulums can help students see a pattern which can be converted to a mathematical formula to determine the period of a pendulum.

The specific gravity of a mineral can be determined by weighing a sample suspended in air, then in water, finding the difference, and dividing the weight in air by that difference.

Social Studies
Data on earthquake locations around the world can be plotted on a map to show the outline of major plates in the Earth's crust as well as familiarize students with the world map. Details for this lesson are included in *Geology: Intermediate* (Young, 1994).

A study of ecology can be extended by looking for signs of changes made by humans on the natural environment around the

> Other subject areas may be used to extend the lessons but should enhance the learning of the science concept.

school grounds and nearby neighborhood. This may include a comparison of native plants and plants found in parks and yards.

Art:
The study of space is fascinating for children and offers the perfect opportunity to develop their creativity in an extender lesson. They can build future space ships and stations from "junk" found around the home.

The beautifully illustrated book *Stellaluna* (Cannon, 1993) can inspire students to write creative science stories and add their own illustrations to bring the stories to life.

Drawings of items which relate to a science study will enhance students' observation skills. If studying cells, these may include microscopic views of one-celled life forms (protozoa) found in pond water, onion skin, or human cheek cells.

Drawings of items which relate to a science study will enhance students' observation skills.

During an assessment and in their science journals, students may be told to include illustrations which will help explain their ideas. This is particularly useful for students whose language arts skills are weak but who can express themselves through art. An example of this is shown on page 22.

Now that you have some background in locating science topics and the structure of individual lessons, the next chapter will help you develop techniques for designing your own science units. You will also find additional lesson ideas in the later chapters of this book.

Phases of the Moon

Question

Why does the moon change its shape?

Setting the Stage

- Have students draw the various shapes they have seen the moon take. Let some of the students draw these examples on the board.
- Ask students to draw what they think happens to change the shape of the moon.
- Tell students this lesson is designed to help them understand the cause of the phases of the moon.

Materials Needed for Each Group

- one set of Moon Phase Cut-outs (see page 19)
- clamp-on light fixture with 150 watt bulb
- 2" (5 cm) styrofoam ball glued to a stick for each student

Procedure

1. Divide students into eight groups and distribute Moon Phase Cut-outs (see page 19).

2. Tell students to assemble the phases in a row in the order of their appearance during a complete cycle.

3. Hang the clamp-on light high at one end of the room, and then darken the room.

4. Have students leave their cutouts at their desks and assemble near the light.

5. Give each student a styrofoam ball on a stick and tell them it represents the moon.

6. Explain to students the ball is the moon, the light is the sun, and their head is the Earth, with their city on the tip of their nose.

7. Turn out the lights and have students watch you as you demonstrate how to create the phases of the moon as follows, turning slowly counterclockwise:
   - New—holding the ball above your head and in front of your face, block out the light.
   - First Quarter—turn 90° from the first position, holding the ball at the same height.
   - Full—turn 180° from the sun, hold the ball above your head and in front of your face.
   - Last Quarter—turn 270° from the first position, holding the ball at the same height.

8. Have students follow your directions as they move, and pause at each phase to examine the shadow of the moon. Be sure they see that the shadow is on the left side of the first quarter and the right side of the last quarter.

9. Let students create the phases of the moon several times in the same sequence. Then, when you feel they are ready, call out a phase for them to show you.

Closure

In their space journals, have students make sets of moon phases showing the correct order from new moon to new moon.

Reprinted from TCM639 Space Intermediate, *Teacher Created Materials, 1994*

Moon Phase Cut-Outs

The moon phases shown below are to be copied to make eight sets. You, as the teacher, should cut these out and number them as separate sets to avoid mixing them. You may wish to enclose each set in an envelope with its number on the outside. Divide students into eight groups and distribute a set of phases to each of them.

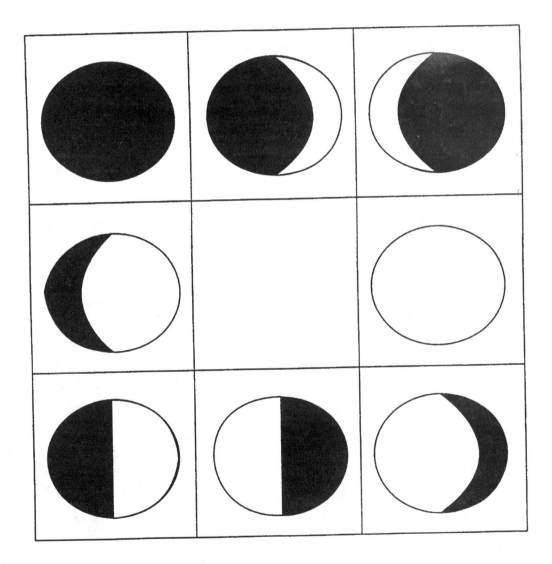

Reprinted from TCM639 Space Intermediate, *Teacher Created Materials, 1994*

Broken Egg

Question
How is the Earth like a hard–boiled egg?

Setting the Stage
- Review with students the layers of the Earth by projecting a transparency of the Earth's layers.
- Tell the students the Earth is like a hard–boiled egg as they will see in this lesson.

Materials Needed for Each Group
- hard–boiled egg
- black tip felt marker
- copy of Earth's Plates, one per student

Procedure
1. Divide students into groups and provide them with their materials.

2. Tell students the Earth's crust is like an egg shell, very thin and brittle.

3. Have students crack the shell around the edge by lightly tapping it on the table. They should not peel off the shell.

4. Ask students to notice how the shell is broken and that some pieces overlap others.

5. Have students use a felt tip pen to carefully outline the edges of the cracked pieces.

6. Explain to students that this is just like the Earth's crust by showing a transparency of the Earth's plates, telling them that these sections of the crust are referred to as plates.

Extensions
- Cut the eggs in half and have each group place a black dot about the size of a pea into the center of the yolk. This represents the inner core of the Earth. Have students look at the thickness of the shell by comparison to that of the rest of the egg and explain that the Earth's crust is actually much thinner relative to the rest of the Earth.

- Have students demonstrate to someone at home how the hard–boiled egg is like the earth. This will enable them to further develop their own understanding of this concept.

Closure
In their geology journals, have students write stories about what it would be like to travel to the center of the Earth.

Reprinted from TCM641 Geology Intermediate, *Teacher Created Materials, 1994*

Cracked Earth

Question
How has the Earth's crust changed?

Setting the Stage
- Remind students of the "Broken Egg" lesson and how the thin crust of the Earth is broken into sections.
- Project for students a transparency of the cracked Earth map and review the different parts.
- Have students use this map to place information collected by scientists to prove the location of the plates.

Materials Needed for Each Group
- one copy of the cracked Earth map for each student
- copy of maps showing the Earth's changes from 200 million years ago to 50 million years in the future for each student
- red, green, and brown crayons or markers
- copy of the Continents Adrift Worksheet for each student
  Note to the teacher: Students will learn the location of the plates which make up the Earth's crust and how scientists have proven the theory of plate tectonics. They will also relate these plates to the shifting of the continents over time.

Procedure
1. Have students examine the cracked Earth map and study the location of the major plates.
2. Have students complete their Continents Adrift Worksheet.
3. Monitor the groups as they work to see that all students participate and ask questions.

Extensions
- Lead students through a comparison of where the plates are located and the changes which have occurred in the Earth's crust during the past 200 million years. Each group should spread their maps in order in front of them and place the cracked Earth map near them. Have students explain what was happening to the plates during these years. They should realize that the Atlantic Ocean floor was spreading apart along the mid-Atlantic ridge. The continents were carried on top of the moving plates to their present locations. The plates will continue to move, and thus the continents will be in a different location 50 million years from now.

- Tell students that the drawings of the past and future locations of the continents are based upon the geological evidence we have today. They may change as we learn more about our Earth.

Reprinted from TCM641 Geology Intermediate, *Teacher Created Materials, 1994*

Introducing Molecules: Response Sheet #1
Experimenting/Observing/Recording Data/Inferring

Name _____ Date _____

This picture shows what the molecules in water might look like if we could see them.

Measure 4 ounces (118 mL) of water. Pour the water into a cup on which the ounces (milliliters) are marked. Measure 2 ounces (56 mL) of sugar. Now you have 4 ounces of water and 2 ounces of sugar, or 6 ounces (174 mL) altogether. Pour the sugar into the water and stir until the sugar dissolves. How many ounces (milliliters) of sugar-water do you have? What happened?

Describe what you think happened when the sugar dissolved in water. Then, on the back of this paper, draw what you think happened.

_____

_____

_____

Reprinted from TCM775 Science Assessment 3–4, *Teacher Created Materials, 1994*

Designing a Unit

What are the components of a science unit?

Once you have discovered the excitement and satisfaction which comes from developing your own science lessons for your students, you are ready to launch into the next step of designing a science unit. A science unit consists of hands-on activity lessons that are linked together in a logical manner. A single lesson is usually completed in one class session of about 30 minutes for students in kindergarten through second grade, 40 minutes for third through fourth grades and 45 to 50 minutes for upper grade students. Each lesson may consist of one or more activities which develop understanding of one science concept. Less is better should be the guide when teaching science. Translated, this means lessons will be more meaningful for students if they cover one idea well to assure understanding, rather than packing bits and pieces of many ideas into each lesson. The brain is somewhat like a sponge; it can only absorb so much new information at a time. When the saturation level is reached, no further learning can take place until the brain has time to "digest" the new information.

> A science unit consists of hands-on activity lessons that are linked together in a logical manner.

There are a variety of ready-made science units and kits commercially available. Some are excellent, while others are of questionable value. Apply the same criteria outlined in the "Getting Started" chapter for evaluating science guides to commercially prepared science units. These units should have a "user friendly" teacher guide with well–written activity lessons that are in a logical sequence. The science kits should supply the necessary materials needed to do the activities. Trade books to extend the science activities should be suggested but, if included in the science kit, should not take the place of science equipment which may be expensive and difficult to obtain. (See the "Resource" section for more information about science kits.)

> There is a certain amount of professional pride in designing your very own science units.

Even the commercially prepared science units require some modification to fit your particular students. Only you, the teacher, know the ability and interest levels of your class. There is a certain amount of professional pride in designing your very own science units. Frequently, ready-made science units will not cover the topics you feel are appropriate for your particular area of the country or for the needs of your students. Students living in Phoenix, far from any ocean, will not benefit much from a study of oceanography, but would from a study of plants and animals of the desert.

There is nothing written that states you may not begin with a ready-made unit and add your own embellishments. You will learn a great deal through this effort and "take ownership" of the finished product.

Should you decide to take up the challenge of designing your own science unit, you will pass through a variety of steps. These are listed below, more or less in the order they occur:

◆ *Selecting the Topic*—you can apply the information on selecting a science topic found in the "Getting Started" chapter to your unit, just as you do for individual lessons.

◆ *Brainstorming*—a period of listing all the ideas and skills you want to teach to the students in this unit.

◆ *Developing Lessons*—writing or finding lessons which teach the ideas you have listed.

◆ *Sequencing Lessons*—put the lessons into a logical order, leading from simple ideas to those which are more complex.

◆ *Locating Materials*—finding or making materials which will be needed for the activities in the unit.

◆ *Developing Assessment*—an important component in the unit which lets you evaluate the knowledge and skills learned as a result of the activities.

◆ *Arranging Study Trips and/or Guest Speakers*—these experiences can enhance and apply student learning. The "Parent Involvement" chapter will provide information on this topic.

◆ *Field Testing*—trying the activities with the students and noting improvements which need to be made.

◆ *Rewriting*—now that the unit has been tested with students, make any improvements needed to make it better.

◆ *Sharing*—after all your hard work of designing this unit, other students should benefit from it. You could offer to teach the unit to more than just your own students or share the unit and supporting materials with other teachers.

Perhaps the most important step of the unit writing process is brainstorming. You will come to know the real meaning of "writer's block" as you attempt to think of the science ideas and skills your students should learn as a result of the unit. Gather plenty of resources from which to glean your lesson ideas. Do not worry if you seem to have too much material at first. You will eliminate those which are not practical or too difficult for your students as you look them over. It may be a good plan to involve another teacher or two to help you write the unit. They can benefit from being part of a professional network and by having a science unit which they helped write to use with their students.

Above all, keep in mind that you are searching for ideas for a science unit, so do not use lessons which fail to develop science concepts or skills.

Check the "Resources" section of this book for suggestions of books which will help you find good lesson ideas. The curriculum and science section of libraries in your school district, neighborhood, or local college are all great places to begin this search. Children's science books such as *Stellaluna* (Cannon, 1993), *The Magic School Bus* series (Cole, 1986ff), and *How to Dig a Hole to the Other Side of the World* (McNulty, 1979) can serve as inspiration for lessons, so comb the bookstores and science museum shops. Be sure to apply the criteria listed on page 10 in the "Getting Started" chapter to any of these materials to avoid getting any which will not be helpful to you.

Above all, keep in mind that you are searching for ideas for a science unit, so do not use lessons which fail to develop science concepts or skills. An example of this would be a leaf rubbing lesson in which a print of the leaf is made by placing it under white paper and rubbing over it with a crayon, charcoal, or pencil. This is an art lesson if the leaves are only used to make attractive prints for a bulletin board. It becomes a science lesson, however, if the prints are used in the ways suggested on the following page.

◆ Examine the imprint of the leaf veins and compare them with those in the human body.

◆ Show damage from insects or diseases.

◆ Compare leaves from various trees.

◆ Sort the leaves by shape and arrangement on a stem.

◆ Compare a variety of leaves from the same tree to see changes which may appear during growth.

◆ Record the rubbings in a notebook throughout a season.

Another example is when a historical study, such as researching the lives of famous astronomers, is mistakenly labeled a science lesson. What do students learn about astronomy through this lesson? This may be a good extender of a study of astronomy, if the study is to reveal the scientific research done by the astronomers. When students view the moon through a telescope, they can appreciate how Galileo Galilei, the Father of Astronomy, felt when he first saw the details on the moon's surface, which no one had ever been able to see before. Visiting a planetarium to watch the motion of planets speeded up to show how they move against the background of stars over many months will help the children understand the work of the great astronomers Tycho Brahe, Johannes Kepler, and Isaac Newton. This makes an otherwise dull study of these ancient astronomers exciting and personal.

When developing science lessons, keep them simple.

When developing science lessons, keep them simple. If they appear complicated, chances are they will be too difficult to conduct and will confuse your students. Some activities will not be practical or safe for your students to conduct and therefore may be done as a demonstration. However, remember that students will learn more if they do the activity than they will by observing someone else do it for them. A demonstration may be used to initiate an activity which students will do immediately after observing it (see the "Getting Started" chapter, page 13, for a demonstration lesson of this type). It may also provide students with a problem to solve by requiring application of ideas which they learned earlier in the unit.

An example of this is a mystery demonstration which can be solved by understanding the basic concepts of magnetism. You will need a strong magnet; the ring magnets which can be purchased at a local electronics store will work well. While students are not in the room, attach the magnet to a bulletin board, then hide it beneath a picture. Suspend a paper clip on a thread near the picture so that it hangs at an angle when placed over the magnet which is hidden by the picture.

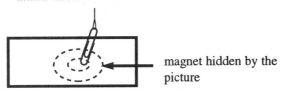

attach thread to bulletin board

magnet hidden by the picture

When the students return to the classroom, let them look at the bulletin board display. Suspend another paper clip from the same location to show them that it hangs straight down, as one would expect. Have each student draw what they think is causing the paper clip to hang at an angle. Tell them to label their drawings and write descriptions of their hypotheses. After they have made their drawings, show them what happens when you place a piece of cardboard between the picture and the paper clip. The paper clip should stick to the cardboard. Ask if this changes their explanations. Let the students share their ideas with the class, then design ways to test them. This example will work well with students following a brief study of magnets. It can also be used to initiate a unit on magnetism or as an assessment item at the end of the unit.

Lessons should be interesting and involve the students in worthwhile activities, leading to a better understanding of the big ideas to be learned in this unit of study. There is no magic number of lessons needed to form a unit; it depends upon the topic, grade level, interests and abilities of the students. It is a good plan not to exhaust the students' interest in a topic, however. Leave them wanting more and they will carry on their own study after the unit ends.

How do I link the lessons together?

By carefully sequencing lessons to fit together in a step-by-step progression, a unit will flow smoothly. Once you find the lessons you want to use in the unit, organize them in a sequence which begins with development of basic information and skills and steadily increases understanding of the subject matter. Deciding what the students will need to know before they do each lesson will help you arrange the proper sequence. If the unit is a study of magnetism the sequence might be as follows:

◆ Sort a variety of materials to designate those which should stick to a magnet. Then test them by using a magnet.
◆ Test classroom items to find which stick to a magnet.
◆ Experiment with magnets to see how they react to each other.

By carefully sequencing lessons to fit together in a step-by-step progression, a unit will flow smoothly.

- ◆ Conduct tests to see if anything can stop magnetism from passing through it.
- ◆ Make a magnetic toy, tool, or magic trick.
- ◆ Conduct a strength test on different types of magnets.
- ◆ Suspend a bar magnet to locate the Earth's magnetic field.
- ◆ Make a compass from a steel pin.
- ◆ Outline the magnetic field of a magnet using iron filings.

These activity lessons are sequenced to provide experience with magnets, which gradually increases the depth of understanding of magnetism. The first few lessons let students explore magnets to literally "get a feel" for how they work. Then students apply this knowledge as they make a magnetic toy, tool, or magic trick. They investigate the Earth's magnetic field and use this information to make a compass. Finally, they bring the magnetic field into view with iron filings. There would be approximately nine or ten lessons in this unit on magnetism.

Extender lessons for the unit can integrate other subjects to enhance learning about the topic. Using the unit on magnetism as an example, students could research the history of magnets to find where they were discovered and how they were first used. They could devise a way to test the strength of magnets using paper clips and collecting data to compare a variety of magnets. Determining the mass each magnet can lift by comparison to its own mass will use mathematics to prove that larger magnets are not always the strongest.

A magnet search at home and elsewhere will show the various uses for magnets, including computers, cassette tapes, speakers, and electric generators. A field trip to a hospital which has a magnetic resonance imaging (MRI) instrument would illustrate the use of a very strong magnetic field to make images of the inside of the body without using harmful X-rays. A visit to a junk yard will show students the use of strong electromagnets.

An art lesson could stem from the activity of outlining the magnetic field with iron filings. You will need sun sensitive paper which is a specially treated paper that fades quickly when exposed to sunlight, except those areas of the paper which are covered. The procedure is to work inside where there is little light, lay a magnet on a tray or cardboard, place the sun sensitive paper over it, then sprinkle iron filings carefully over the paper. Now, expose all of this to bright sunlight until the paper fades. Carry the materials out of the sunlight, dump the iron filings off the paper and submerge the paper in water

These activity lessons are sequenced to provide experience with magnets, which gradually increases the depth of understanding of magnetism.

to set the image. You will have a picture of the magnetic field left by the shadow of the filings. These make an interesting bulletin board display or greeting cards, while illustrating the magnetic field of the magnet.

Lessons on orienteering (finding your directions relative to north) would not only extend the understanding of how magnetism helps us but applies simple geometry while developing this useful skill. Orienteering requires the use of a liquid filled compass, which is very accurate. The magnetized needle of this compass moves on a pivot point in a clear liquid which is encased in plastic. A dial marked off in 360° degrees is turned to the bearing (direction) you want to go, such as 0° for north, 90° for east, 180° for south, 270° for west, or any points in between these settings. The magnetic needle always points north, thus enabling the person using the compass to have a fixed point to help set his or her correct bearing and move in that direction. For example, if you wanted to walk 320°, you would set the compass to look like the one below:

The "Resources" section of this book has a list of mail order science suppliers.

Direction: 320°

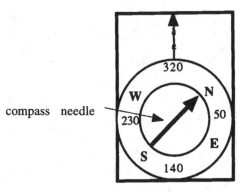

compass needle

The "Resources" section of this book has a list of mail order science suppliers. They will be glad to send you free catalogs on request, and your name will be placed on mailing lists for future catalogs. These companies frequently offer discounts when you order multiples of a particular item. Some of the suppliers carry live specimens, such as Painted Lady Butterfly larva, or silkworm eggs, or ants available from Insect Lore. Various protozoa may be ordered from Carolina Biological Supply Co. (see their address listed beside Science and Technology for Children in the "Resources" section).

Most of these companies will accept school district purchase order numbers or credit card numbers. This often speeds up the delivery process if you need materials in a hurry. Their customer service representatives can be reached by telephone and will assist you in placing your order.

Science materials mentioned in this chapter, such as orienteering compasses, are available in nature and camping supply stores, but can also be ordered from Edmund Scientific and Delta Education. Sun sensitive paper is carried by Insect Lore (they call it nature print paper), and iron filings may be purchased from Edmund Scientific.

A very important part of your hands-on science unit will be appropriate assessment. The next chapter describes a variety of ways to assess the level of understanding and skills your students have attained.

Assessment Alternatives

How can I assess hands-on science activities?

Sometimes the students are having so much fun with their science activities that you begin to doubt they are really learning anything. When you design each lesson, make a note of the concepts and skills you expect the students to learn as a result of the activities they will be doing. The science lessons your students will experience emphasize conceptual learning and skill development rather than the memorization of science facts. Traditional methods of assessment such as multiple choice, true/false, or completion questions which check for recall of facts and vocabulary are totally inadequate for assessing your students' progress.

The assessments you use should directly relate to the lessons and evaluate students' conceptual understanding and skill development, as well as the effectiveness of the lessons. The advantage to using multiple forms of assessment is that they will generate a variety of information to help create a valid picture of each student's progress and abilities. Examples of methods for assessing student learning from hands-on science lessons are listed on the next page.

> The science lessons your students will experience emphasize conceptual learning and skill development rather than the memorization of science facts.

◆ *Teacher observations*—made as students work individually or in groups

◆ *Science journals*—kept by students as they study a variety of science topics

◆ *Open-ended questions*—questions which have a variety of acceptable answers

◆ *Enhanced multiple choice*—questions which may involve a display of items or ask students to explain their answers to a multiple choice question

◆ *Performance based questions*—questions which are answered by performing an activity

◆ *Portfolios*—collection of samples of each student's work to record academic growth over an extended period of time

Teacher Observations

Teacher observations can be done using a checklist of the skills related to each lesson and evaluating the students as they work individually or in groups. Look at the list of science process skills described in the "Overview" chapter and add those which fit the lesson or unit being evaluated to the checklist. Group skills such as cooperating and contributing good ideas should also be evaluated. You may wish to use a ranking system to indicate the level of each student such as 1–5, with 5 being the highest level. Examples of teacher observation checklists are shown in *Science Assessment*: *Grades 3–4*, (Jasmine, 1994).

Teacher observations may also include an anecdotal record on individuals. An example of such a record form is shown on page 37. This record can be modified for individual assessment and become a piece of the total evaluation of each student's abilities and progress.

Science Journals

Students can maintain science journals that may be used to record observations, data, or results of experiments. Drawings as well as written entries may be included in the journals. Entries on magnetism might include drawings showing observations of how two magnets interact, how a compass works, or prints from the iron filing lesson showing the magnetic field.

Students may be asked to write an evaluation of a lesson including what they enjoyed, learned, and would like to learn. The teacher may use the science journal as a means of checking student understanding and getting input regarding the success of a lesson or assessing the level of interest to continue the topic.

Students can maintain science journals that may be used to record observations, data, or results of experiments.

Open-Ended Questions

This type of evaluation can be used as a unique way to have students demonstrate the depth of their understanding of concepts being taught. An example of an open-ended question related to the magnetism unit follows.

You have suddenly been turned into a human magnet. Describe in detail how this will change the things you can do and what problems you may have now that you are magnetic. Make a drawing of yourself as a human magnet and label the drawing to explain its parts.

As you can see, this question can be answered in many ways, but you are checking for understanding of the concepts of magnetism from the unit which are:

The conceptual understanding each student has will be clearly illustrated in his or her answer to the open-ended question.

◆ Magnets will stick to things made of iron, nickel, and cobalt but not to any other metals.

◆ Magnetism travels long distances (e.g., the earth's magnetism).

◆ Magnetism can be used to help find directions.

◆ Magnetism passes through nearly everything, including flesh and bone.

◆ Magnets vary in strength. The strongest magnets are electromagnets.

◆ Magnets have poles. When two magnets are brought close together, poles which are alike will repel and opposite poles will attract.

◆ Magnets are surrounded by a magnetic field which arcs between the positive and negative poles.

◆ Magnetism is an energy force which is very useful to people.

The conceptual understanding each student has will be clearly illustrated in his or her answer to the open-ended question. The drawing will assist those who are not proficient with words by permitting them to show their knowledge through an illustration.

Grading this type of assessment activity is more of a challenge, requiring that each student's work be examined carefully and assigned points on the basis of thoroughness of explanation, as well as grasp of the concepts. It is best to look at all the students' work before deciding on individual scores. You will get a better idea of students' reactions to the question, helping you determine how much to expect from them before developing the scoring system for this particular assessment.

Enhanced Multiple Choice

It is effective and often enjoyable to employ a display when assessing science skills and understanding. The magnetism unit provides an opportunity to set out a display of materials used in one of the early activities to show what items would be picked up by a magnet. Spread these over a table and label each one with a letter. Give the students a record sheet which asks them to circle the letters of items which a magnet would pick up. The multiple choice question becomes enhanced when the students are asked to defend their answers. Ask them why they chose the items they circled. This will check to be sure that they understood the concept and were not just guessing the answers. An additional check for understanding and another method of enhancement would be to have the students give two examples of things that are not included in the display which would stick to a magnet.

> The multiple choice question becomes enhanced when the students are asked to defend their answers.

Performance-Based Questions

This type of question involves doing an activity to reach an answer. Students often find performance-based assessment fun, yet it clearly demonstrates the skills and knowledge which they have gained through the activities in the lesson unit. Examples of performance-based questions related to magnetism follow.

1. Invent a test to find which magnet is the strongest. Make a detailed sketch of your test and label the parts of the drawing.

2. Make a magnetic toy. Draw the toy and show how it works.

There should be three or four activities which the students perform alone or in pairs. The materials provide them the opportunity to experiment before answering the question. Materials for each question can be spread out on desks or tables which are screened for privacy by using cardboard walls to divide the work areas. If multiple centers are set up, students can rotate from station to station, at a given signal, until they have completed each of the tasks.

The teacher can evaluate the students' skills by observing them as they work and completing a checklist containing the skills which are related to the activities, as well as making notes about the degree of understanding each child is demonstrating. The answer sheets can be scored much the same as the open-ended questions are. Performance-based assessment is a powerful way to evaluate student progress and the value of the completed activity lessons.

Portfolios

This system of assessment is a collection of student work over a period of time to show growth. The materials can be collected in a folder, box, or envelope for each child. Selection of materials to include should be at the discretion of the teacher for young students. One of the goals of this system is to help students develop techniques for evaluating their own work. They should be able to update their own portfolios, under the guidance of the teacher at first until they develop the skills to do this for themselves. The materials in the portfolio are useful during teacher-student and teacher-parent conferences to demonstrate the child's learning progress. Concrete examples of the student's work are far more effective than comments made by the teacher.

A videotape record or photographs of the students' activities as they work may be included in a portfolio. This could be applied to the study of magnetism by taping some of the early activities with magnets, then adding observations of more advanced activities to show individual student growth, as well as that of the class as a whole. Students could view the videotape with the teacher to help them develop their skills of self-evaluation.

One of the goals of this system is to help students develop techniques for evaluating their own work.

Scoring Alternative Assessment

Scoring alternative assessment is more challenging than typical objective tests which assess only factual knowledge. The alternative assessment techniques check for conceptual understanding, offer opportunities to apply knowledge, and check the student's ability to think and perform at various levels. The scoring technique for alternative assessment is done by applying a rubric, or scale of achievement. The scale can be based upon a score of 0–4, with number 4 being the highest level. Levels of performance are assigned to each number. Below is an example of a rubric scale.

4 points—Outstanding:
  Clearly demonstrates complete understanding of the important concepts and is accurate.

3 points—Very Good:
  Generally shows understanding of the important concepts but may omit a few details, yet it is accurate.

2 points—Adequate:
  Shows some understanding and accuracy, but is incomplete.

1 point—Inadequate:
  Does not understand the concepts and is inaccurate.

Another rubric example is provided on page 38.

Assessment is undergoing the same revision as teaching methods, moving from rote memory to direct involvement of the students physically and mentally in the learning process. The October, 1994 issue of *Science and Children* is devoted to alternative assessment articles written by teachers and experts on this subject. Details and many helpful examples are provided for each of the various forms of assessment. This journal may be ordered from the National Science Teachers Association (NSTA). See the "Resource" section of this book for the address of NSTA. *Science and Children* may also be available at your local library or school district office.

The rewards of applying the current assessment techniques are well worth the time and efforts of the teacher and students.

As you try some of the new methods of assessment, be patient with yourself and your students. It takes time to become accustomed to assessing understanding of knowledge and progress in skill development through the various forms of assessment. The rewards of applying the current assessment techniques are well worth the time and efforts of the teacher and students. Work with other teachers to help develop these new techniques and exchange ideas and suggestions.

Teaching hands-on science requires more stuff than the traditional method of using a textbook. The chapter which follows provides ideas for management of the classroom and science materials.

Anecdotal Records for Groups

Example

Members of Group: Date _12/10/94_

Bill Jones   _Rhan Ng_

Samantha Edwards   _Shawnella Green_

Julio Gonzoles   _____

Skill(s) Being Observed:

Students were classifying the data they collected about clouds.

Comments:

They need more practice in listening to each other. Good ideas were being expressed, but not everyone was willing to listen.

Reprinted from TCM775 Science Assessment: Grades 3–4, _Teacher Created Materials, 1994_

Reliable Assessment

Observation-Based Assessment

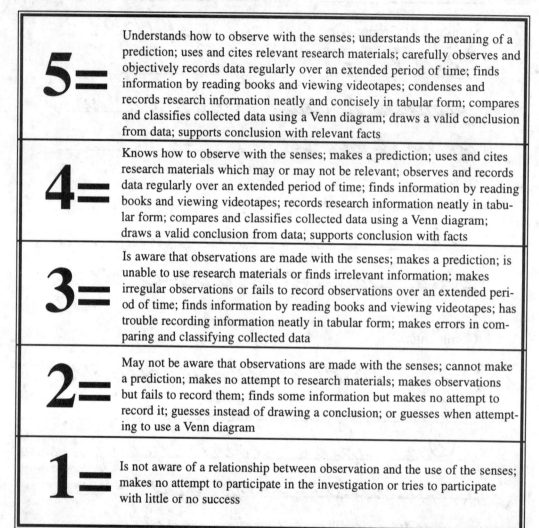

5 = Understands how to observe with the senses; understands the meaning of a prediction; uses and cites relevant research materials; carefully observes and objectively records data regularly over an extended period of time; finds information by reading books and viewing videotapes; condenses and records research information neatly and concisely in tabular form; compares and classifies collected data using a Venn diagram; draws a valid conclusion from data; supports conclusion with relevant facts

4 = Knows how to observe with the senses; makes a prediction; uses and cites research materials which may or may not be relevant; observes and records data regularly over an extended period of time; finds information by reading books and viewing videotapes; records research information neatly in tabular form; compares and classifies collected data using a Venn diagram; draws a valid conclusion from data; supports conclusion with facts

3 = Is aware that observations are made with the senses; makes a prediction; is unable to use research materials or finds irrelevant information; makes irregular observations or fails to record observations over an extended period of time; finds information by reading books and viewing videotapes; has trouble recording information neatly in tabular form; makes errors in comparing and classifying collected data

2 = May not be aware that observations are made with the senses; cannot make a prediction; makes no attempt to research materials; makes observations but fails to record them; finds some information but makes no attempt to record it; guesses instead of drawing a conclusion; or guesses when attempting to use a Venn diagram

1 = Is not aware of a relationship between observation and the use of the senses; makes no attempt to participate in the investigation or tries to participate with little or no success

Use Your Own Judgement

Remember that the most important thing elementary school students will be learning as they do their investigations is how to investigate. The skills necessary for the process are the ones you will be developing and assessing.

Reprinted from TCM775 Science Assessment: Grades 3–4, *Teacher Created Materials, 1994*

Management Tips

Should students work in groups or individually?

The type of science lesson being conducted will dictate whether students should work individually, as a whole class, or in groups of two to four. The nature of the lesson may change as it is being taught, necessitating more than one way to group the students. For instance, if students are viewing a film to provide science background for an activity, obviously they will see it as a whole class. This will change, however, if the teacher makes the film content valuable by previewing the film and writing some thought provoking questions that students will be asked to think about as they watch the movie. The students should be told they will be responsible for discussing the answers in small groups at the end of the film. The grouping for this lesson, therefore, uses large group, individual, and cooperative group instruction.

It is generally better to have students do hands-on activities in small groups since less equipment is required and, like scientists, they can benefit from the exchange of ideas. Groups should have no more than four members so each child has an opportunity to participate in

The type of science lesson being conducted will dictate whether students should work individually, as a whole class, or in groups of two to four.

the discussion and activity. The requirements of the lesson will determine the skill levels needed in each group and thus dictate whether students can be assigned at random or must have a balance of ability levels. It is also a good idea not to keep the same groups together for every lesson. However, if the activity is spread over time in order to observe and collect data (such as the changes of plants or butterfly larva as they grow), the same students may need to work together throughout the entire study.

When students are working in groups, make certain that no member is excluded from the activity. This may be done in a variety of ways as shown below:

When students are working in groups, make certain that no member is excluded from the activity.

- ◆ Students number off around their table and the teacher assigns responsibilities for each number.
- ◆ Rotate the responsibility during the activity so each member of the group has equal opportunity.
- ◆ If students are asked to discuss something, give them thinking time, then have the students count off in the group. Tell them to begin with number one and take turns sharing their answers.

This division of labor assures that each member of the class is participating and that no one dominates or withdraws from the group. It is also more likely that students will be willing to share their ideas with a small group than with the entire class, since this is less intimidating.

The teacher has the perfect opportunity to circulate among the groups as they work and discuss, listening to the students' contributions and assessing their thinking skills as well as their ability to work cooperatively. See the previous chapter on "Assessment Alternatives" for details on how to do this assessment.

Be alert to any statements which show misinterpretations of concepts so they can be corrected later. An example of a misconception is: "Moisture appears on the outside of a glass of ice water because the water molecules are squeezing through the glass." The correct interpretation of this observation is that moisture is formed by moisture in the air coming in contact with the cold glass and condensing (clinging) to the outside of the glass.

Chances are, if one student has a misconception, others may also. It is usually best to wait until the students are finished with their discussion then diplomatically mention the misconception and explain the correct interpretation.

Will science activities be noisy?

One of the major concerns for some teachers who are beginning to teach hands-on science is that the students will not be working in silence. There is no doubt these lessons will not be quiet, but the noise should be that which results from students interacting with each other to perform a task. Think of a task you have performed such as yard work, hanging pictures, packing boxes, or cooking a meal. These all generate a certain amount of noise, but it is necessary to get the job done. The same is true for science activities. Students should be required to keep their noise to a minimum as they work; however, absolute silence will hamper their learning.

Conversation between students is also a necessary part of working cooperatively. The teacher needs to monitor the class by walking among the students to be sure their discussion is about the subject being studied. If they appear to be conducting "social" conversations, it is time to check with the group to see if they have completed their assignment. Just the presence and awareness of the teacher is usually sufficient to remind students of their responsibilities. Of course, it is important that assignments be of value and clearly explained or confusion and inattentiveness may result. After giving instructions, watch to see that students begin their work. If they appear not to understand what is expected of them, ask all students to stop working so you may give additional instructions.

Students should be required to keep their noise to a minimum as they work; however, absolute silence will hamper their learning.

If instructions are somewhat complex, give them in short segments. Write the steps on the board or on a transparency for an overhead projector so students can refer to them as they work. Ask for a few students to repeat the instructions aloud if you want to check their comprehension. Always permit time for questions from the students after you give instructions and prior to beginning the lesson. Students may become inventive and change the instructions for their own needs. This is acceptable as long as they are accomplishing the goal you have set for them.

Groups do not all finish at the same time, so be prepared to provide those who finish early with an activity that will keep them occupied. Some of the options for this time may be reading science magazines or trade books, or quietly looking at science displays in the classroom. The "Resources" section lists examples of science magazines and books appropriate for elementary students. Should the principal or other visitors come to your classroom during a science lesson, take time to explain the science activity to them and invite them to participate. They will see the value of the students' work and understand why it cannot be done in silence.

How do I handle all the "science stuff"?

The drawback to hands-on science is all the materials needed to do the activities. This calls for organization to avoid the desire to make science less work by using a textbook, which changes the study from science to language arts. Plan ahead for each lesson to have the materials on hand and ready for distribution. One of the easiest methods to distribute the materials for an activity is to use cafeteria trays. Place the materials needed by each group on the trays and have them ready at the beginning of the lesson. Students can pick up the tray for their groups, then deliver it to a designated location at the end of the class. This makes delivery and cleanup much easier and gives the students responsibility for their own work area.

Plan ahead for each lesson to have the materials on hand and ready for distribution.

Enlist the students' help in making sure all equipment is returned in good condition. Be aware that some materials, such as magnets, may disappear unless a monitoring system is established. One way to do this is to put a list of the materials on file cards for each tray so students can check to see that everything is there before returning it.

As your science units are developed and materials are collected to support that unit, store them in a large plastic container with a lid. These containers should be strong enough to let you stack them. Be sure to label the topic on the sides and top so you can easily find the one you need. Select a container which is large enough to permit adding new materials as you expand the unit. You may want to make a list of the contents to attach inside the lid of the container. This is a good idea if you plan to loan the science kits to other teachers. They are more likely to return the kit intact if the contents list is attached to the box to remind them of the materials which should be inside.

The custom made science kits you develop should contain all the materials you need to do that particular unit. These may include related reference material, related children's books, and periodicals. Be sure to include your detailed lesson plans so they will be ready the next time you teach the topic. Each time you teach the unit, update the materials and lesson plans as you find better ways to teach it.

Organization is the key to providing hands-on science in the classroom. Teaching hands-on science is a lot like preparing, serving, and cleaning up after a meal. The lessons are easier to teach if you maintain a system for storing the materials you need for the unit activities in one place and develop simple classroom techniques for distributing and collecting the science supplies. Your reward will be in the satisfaction of presenting exciting activities that leave your students wanting to learn more about science.

Parent Involvement

How can science extend to the families?

Now that the students are excited about hands-on science, they are most likely interested in sharing their enthusiasm with their families. Several techniques can be used to provide involvement of the students' families in science experiences which relate to the units being conducted in the classroom.

Science Kits on Loan

Teacher created simple science kits may be checked out for several days or a week by individual students. These activities are more effective if they are extenders of a science topic being studied by the class. This is a great way to help students reinforce their knowledge on their own and discover the rewards of teaching others. Science in a Bag and Shoebox Science are examples of these take home kits.

Science in a Bag

Science in a Bag is a series of short activities which can be contained in a large, heavy duty plastic bag. All the materials a student needs to do the activity are provided. Enough supplies may be

> Teacher created simple science kits may be checked out for several days or a week by individual students.

included so the student and another member of his or her family can be involved in the activity. The materials in the bag can include small science books or science periodicals such as *Zoobooks* (Wildlife Education, 1987+) which students can read to gain science knowledge in an easy manner. The science activity should relate directly to the literature. Place a letter inside the bag to tell the parent(s) about the kit, list its contents, and state when it is to be returned to school. A model for the letter is shown below:

Science in a Bag
(Sample Parent Letter)

Dear (Parents),

Family members are encouraged to get involved in this activity, letting the child serve as teacher.

This science kit is on loan to (child's name) to enable him/her to conduct a simple science activity at home. Family members are encouraged to get involved in this activity, letting the child serve as teacher. Class time has been reserved on (date/time) for your child to share the results of this take-home activity. You are welcome to attend his/her presentation.

Examples of two Science in a Bag take-home lessons are as follows:

Owl Pellets
Include a copy of *Owls* (Zoobooks, 1987+) which colorfully and accurately relates interesting and easy to understand information about these predatory birds. This booklet describes owl pellets, which are undigested bones and hair which the owl, like any bird of prey, has to spit out. This is done in the form of pellets, which vary in size depending upon the owl and the meal. The pellets are available in the wild or may be purchased commercially from supply stores such as Insect Lore (see "Resources"). Literature, including bone identification sheets, can also be ordered along with the pellets. Owl pellets are veritable treasure chests, yielding tiny bones from rodents and birds and insect legs, all remains of food eaten by these birds.

The bag should contain the booklet *Owls*, an owl pellet, two toothpicks, a pair of tweezers, and two or three pairs of surgical gloves (available in most drug stores). Add a small bottle of white glue and large file card so students can make a display of the bones. Also place a bone identification sheet inside the bag. Instructions for the students follow on the next page.

- Soak the pellet in warm water for about 10 minutes, to loosen the bones.
- Wear the gloves and work over newspaper.
- Pull the pellet apart with your fingers and use the tweezers and toothpick to separate the bones.
- Hold the bones with the tweezers and wash them in a cup of water to loosen any fur which is stuck to them. Use a toothpick to remove packed fur from tiny holes in the bones.
- Soak the bones for about half an hour in a small cup of water to which a tablespoon (15mL) of bleach has been added.
- Rinse the bones with clean water, lay them on a paper towel or newspaper, and let them dry for 24 hours.
- Sort the bones according to their shapes and lay them side by side on the cardboard in groups of bones which are alike.
- Cover each group of bones with a drop of white glue. (Do not worry; the glue will be clear when it dries so the bones will be visible.)
- Identify the bones using the identification sheet and carefully print the name of the bones below each group.
- Neatly print "Bones from one owl pellet" and your name at the top of the card.
- After the glue has dried for 24 hours, you can place the card of bones inside a heavy plastic bag to protect them.
- Bring your bones to school to display in our classroom.

The contents of an owl pellet make a wonderful study of anatomy.

The bone display can be returned to school and used to estimate the number of animals represented in the pellet by counting the skulls or the bones which come in pairs, such as the jaw, shoulder blade, or pelvis.

Another way of mounting the bones is to glue them to a drawing of the skeleton of a rat, which is frequently a food source of owls. These drawings are usually included with the information you purchase along with the pellets. Although not all the bones will be found, nor will they match in size those in the drawing, this activity will show the students the location of the bones. The size of an animal can also be estimated by looking at the skull or leg bones. The contents of an owl pellet make a wonderful study of anatomy.

Dinosaurs

A copy of *Dinosaurs: A Journey Through Time* (Schatz, 1987) can be used to create several Science in a Bag kits. This book is filled with information about dinosaurs, including recent discoveries. Throughout this paperback book are cut-out or punch-out activities which include the following:

- ♦ Match the Dinosaur—a card game of matching the dinosaur description to its picture.
- ♦ What's It For?—a card game which matches pictures of modern-day objects to body parts of dinosaurs, such as the horns of Triceratops to a sword and the foot of Tyrannosaurus Rex (T Rex) to that of an ostrich.
- ♦ Punch-out bones of Triceratops and T Rex to assemble are also included in this book.

Each bag can include the materials needed to play one of the games or assemble one of the dinosaurs. Other members of the family can easily participate. A copy of the related dinosaur information from the book can be enclosed with the game. It is a good idea to laminate the game pieces, cardboard "bones," and literature for durability.

Permitting time for students to share their take-home activities with the class will add value to their work and act as an incentive to do their best work. If a date and time for the report to the class is designated on the parent letter, there will be more likelihood that the task will be completed and the kit will be returned for the next student to check out.

Shoebox Science

Shoebox Science take-home kits are similar to Science in a Bag but contain larger items and therefore require a sturdy box. All the instructions and supplies needed for a science project to be conducted by the student, along with family members, are placed in the kit. A letter to the parents should be included. Use the one from Science in a Bag as a model. Examples of Shoebox Science kits follow.

Electricity

This kit should be used after the students have experimented with D-cell batteries, 2.5 volt light bulbs, and wire to construct simple circuits. It lets them apply their skills and knowledge of basic electricity. A kit containing the materials needed to construct a flashlight will provide this experience. These are listed on the following page.

Shoebox Science take-home kits are similar to Science in a Bag but contain larger items and therefore require a sturdy box.

46

- Two D-cell batteries
- Two eight inch lengths (20 cm) of coated 22 gauge wire (telephone wire) with the insulation stripped off the ends
- One 2.5 volt flashlight bulb and socket
- An empty toilet paper roll or a piece of thin cardboard
- A roll of masking tape
- Piece of aluminum foil about 8" (20 cm) x 10" (25 cm)

Student Instructions:
Using the materials in this kit, make a flashlight which can be turned off and on. Make a drawing of your flashlight to explain how it works. Bring your flashlight and drawing back to school to share with the class on (date).

Magnetism
Following a series of lessons where students use a variety of magnets to discover their properties, they are now ready to apply this learning by creating a magnetic toy, trick, or tool. Suggestions for materials to be included in this kit are:

- Various magnets from which to choose
- Roll of masking tape
- 12" (30 cm) of string
- Small box

Student Instructions:
Use any materials in this kit, and those you may have at home, to make a magnetic toy, trick, or tool. You may ask for help from your family, but you should design your invention and do most of the work. We are looking forward to seeing your invention on (date), when you will get to share it with our class.

Family Science

Conducting a Family Science Night will extend the joy of experiencing science activities to the families and create a bond between parents and children. The objective of this event is to give the parents an opportunity to experience the science activities in which their children have been involved. Since parents and children are invited to participate together, it is usually best to schedule this occasion on an evening to accommodate working parents. Once they have shared the excitement of these activities with their children, they will be very supportive of your efforts. The children also benefit by being able to work with their parents to show them what they have learned in their science classes.

Conducting a Family Science Night will extend the joy of experiencing science activities to the families and create a bond between parents and children.

If the students are in the primary grades, the teacher will need to take the responsibility of deciding what activities the parents and their children will do together. If older students are involved, they can be prepared to act as instructors for their parents. Select a variety of science activities which the students have done in class and let them choose one or more they want to teach to their parents. You may want to choose only one activity which will be done by everyone in small cooperative groups, just as you do in the science classes.

If you decide to offer more than one activity, it is a good idea to use only three or four so they are easier to manage. Multiple stations for each activity may be set up and participants can rotate through them, like learning centers in a classroom. Establish a signal for stopping an activity such as clapping three times, a pleasant sounding bell, or recorded music. Allow sufficient time for each group to do their activity, then signal them to stop and clean up their center. Explain before they move how each group is to rotate to the next center. Numbering the centers will organize the rotation system.

Select a variety of science activities which the students have done in class and let them choose one or more they want to teach to their parents.

Family Science Night may be successful beyond your wildest dreams so be prepared for a crowd. Send home an announcement which contains a reservation form for this special event so you will know how many to prepare for and what room arrangements are necessary. If you receive an overwhelming response, plan two nights and ask parents to choose which is better for them or move into a larger room. Request the help of several reliable parents. Have some come early to help with the setup and another group to remain for the cleanup. There may also be another teacher or two who would be interested in participating in a joint Family Science Night. Give some thought to the possibility of having older students take the responsibility for teaching their parents as well as younger students and their parents. This would be a great way to lay the seeds for future teachers and bolster the egos of these student scientists.

Check with your school's parent support group and district office personnel to encourage their participation and attendance. This will hopefully lead to increased interest in your science program and may even provide you with future resources in the way of volunteers and funding. Be sure to let the local news media know about your Family Science Night; the public needs to know the positive aspects of today's educational programs.

Parents as Partners
Invite the parents to become partners with you in the effort to teach meaningful science. Send home a letter early in the school year to

inform the parents of the science topics you plan to cover and encourage them to participate. This may be as simple as loaning science books, materials, or interesting science displays to the class. There may also be parents who have careers in science, or know of friends or relatives who do, and are willing to come to school and share their work with the students. This may even lead to a field trip to their place of business.

Ask parents to volunteer in the classroom during science classes to assist you with the work involved in preparing and conducting science activities. If this can be done on a scheduled basis, you will be able to train the parents and improve their skills as aides and as instructors for their own children. This partnership between teacher and parents will enhance children's learning since they will receive reinforcement for their efforts as their parents observe their work.

Should I take my class on science study trips?

Science field trips add enrichment when they relate directly to the science topics being studied in the classroom. There are really three parts to any field trip: preparation before going, participation during the trip, and the culmination of the experiences and knowledge gleaned. Each of these aspects is equally important and needs to be well planned in order to take full advantage of this unique opportunity. It will also demonstrate to the students how they can make the most of any travel experience, thus developing skills which can be applied when they travel with their families or later in life. Suggestions for assuring a successful trip are as follows:

Preparation:
◆ Conduct activities that give the science background needed to enhance understanding during the field experience.

If the trip is to be a marine science cruise, familiarize students with the sea life they are likely to see, as well as the instruments they may use on board, such as sampling devices.

If students will be visiting a large museum, narrow the focus to only a portion of the exhibits and provide the students with background that will enable them to go with some advance knowledge of what they will be viewing.

Show slides which describe the trip for the students so they will be informed participants and can look forward to the experience.

Science field trips add enrichment when they relate directly to the science topics being studied in the classroom.

◆ Design activities that begin in the classroom but require data or ideas gathered during the trip to complete.

Visiting an estuary in winter and spring offers a great opportunity for students to conduct a bird count and a survey of the different species they see. The classroom activities can include learning how to use bird identification cards and developing methods for recording the types and number of birds observed. This data can serve as the basis for comparing the difference in bird life in the area during the culmination activities following the two trips.

Taking a marine science trip will yield data regarding the ocean water and organisms collected for study on the ship. This data may be in the form of drawings of plankton, fish, and other sea life collected, as well as the pH value of the sea water and the temperature at various depths.

◆ Involve students in planning the trip by letting them use a map to locate where they are going and determine the distance they will travel.

Divide the route of the trip into sections and assign groups of students the responsibility of researching their portion of a map for the entire route and highlighting points of interest.

Make copies of the maps for each group and have them highlight the route as well as the points of interest they should watch for during the trip.

During the ride to the study trip site, have students navigate by following the route of the bus or car on their map and marking off the points of interest as they see them.

Participation

Preview the study trip before your students go and prepare questions for them to answer which will use higher level thinking skills, rather than just searching for facts. Contact the site of the study trip to see if they have curriculum materials which may be used for the trip. Some examples of ways the teacher can have the students gather information while on the field trip are listed below:

◆ If the trip is to an area such as a zoo, estuary, or natural setting, have students observe one or two of the animals they see and write notes describing the behavior, sounds, and physical characteristics they observe. Ask them to give examples of how this animal has physically adapted to its environment (i.e., heavy fur, long claws, flexible toes).

> **Preview the study trip before your students go and prepare questions for them to answer which will use higher level thinking skills, rather than just searching for facts.**

- Drawings will help students look for details, but they should concentrate on only a few things to sketch and describe or label their illustrations.

- Create a "scavenger hunt" which applies to the area being visited to enable students to look for specific details that relate to the topic being studied. Make this game more than "fill in the facts" by asking them to find unusual things such as bird feathers at an estuary or animal foot prints along wildlife trails. If they are visiting a museum, ask questions which direct them to look closer at selected exhibits to narrow their field of concentration and thus improve the chances of learning in depth.

- Consider taking one or more video cameras if the visit is to an outdoor site. Have the students develop a video record of their trip, narrating it as they go, then editing the videotape for a presentation to parents after the trip. Plan an outline of what will be taped in advance of the trip so students will make a valuable record of their experiences rather than one which randomly documents events. Provide students with a map of the study field site so they can plot their route and decide on what they will tape.

Culmination

Experiences during the culmination of the study trip should complete the loop by tying together the activities done in the classroom and the data gathered on the trip. This can be done in a variety of methods, depending upon what the activities were in the preparation stage. Examples of using the data are shown below:

- If students were asked to gather data regarding the type and number of birds at an estuary, the data can be graphed to compare the two seasons. It is important to analyze the data in order to make it of value. A series of questions, such as those shown below, will help students in this activity.

  When were there more birds at the estuary, in the winter or spring?

  Why were there different birds when we came in the winter than in the spring?

  Compare the sizes of the birds. Were there more large or small birds? Explain why this happens.

- Review the scavenger hunt list and have students describe what they learned to the group. They should also write a summary of their experiences and new knowledge in their *Science Journals*.

> Create a "scavenger hunt" which applies to the area being visited to enable students to look for specific details that relate to the topic being studied.

◆ Drawings made by students during the trip should be displayed in the classroom and later be included in their journals.

◆ If a videotape was made of the trip, have students review it and concentrate on adding narration about what they learned. Give them the incentive to do a good job of this by telling them the videotape will be used during a meeting with their parents to show what they did on the trip. A videotape of the classroom science activities done in the preparation stage for the study trip can be included with that of the trip to form a complete history of the experience.

Encourage parents to join the class on field trips. They will realize the value of this experience and appreciate your skills as a teacher. They can also see their own children as they interact with their peers. This enables the parents to see the behavior patterns you have observed in the classroom, which are often different from those they see at home. Be sure to invite the parents to attend the preparation and culminating sessions provided for the students.

How can I make use of local resources?

Do not overlook the wealth of materials which are available to teachers through local libraries, museums, colleges, and science facilities. Frequently, these facilities will offer curriculum which has been written for teachers and which is free or relatively inexpensive. Place your name on the mailing lists of these institutions to receive notices of events which will yield possible study trips or opportunities for you to further develop your science background.

You may contact the local service organizations, such as Kiwanis, Soroptimist, and science associations that may be willing to fund your attendance at a conference or science course. Offer to be a guest speaker to share your experience at one of their meetings or write an article for their newsletter in exchange for the financial support.

If funds are needed for science materials or study trips are needed for students, this may be available through these same groups, as well as your school's parent support group. The students should show their appreciation for this assistance by writing thank you notes that include information about their experiences. You may also want to invite representatives of the group to visit the class or have some of the students go to one of their meetings so students can personally share how they benefited from the contribution.

Do not overlook the wealth of materials which are available to teachers through local libraries, museums, colleges, and science facilities.

Check with the high school science teachers to see whether they have equipment they can loan you, such as microscopes, dissecting instruments, or chemicals. Be sure you ask the science teachers to show you how to use the equipment if you are not familiar with it. They will be more likely to agree to loan their materials if you set a date for its return and assure them that you will return it in the same condition it is in when you receive it. If the items loaned to you are not returned in time or are damaged, borrowing privileges will no doubt be withdrawn.

Science related companies such as research labs and hospitals may have materials which they are willing to donate to your class. These may include X-rays, equipment, preserved specimens, or science pictures worthy of being displayed on your bulletin boards. They may also be willing to let your students tour their facilities.

Consider having guest speakers visit your class to highlight different science careers. Speakers may be available from local industries, science museums, and science departments at colleges and universities. This opportunity will expand the students' vision of possible career goals. It is best to initiate this at upper elementary levels, thus permitting time for students to make the academic choices necessary to prepare for a science career.

Ask the speaker to share with the class pictures or materials which will help them understand what is involved in the career and what training is required. Prepare the students several days before the guests arrive by providing brief description of their careers and having students think of questions they may wish to ask. It may be wise to send the questions in advance to the speakers so they can be ready to respond.

Let the students suggest professions they are interested in learning about and, if possible, find speakers who represent those careers. Visiting the professionals at their places of business is often even more effective, since they can demonstrate what they do and show the connection to science.

Forming partnerships between your school and a local science museum, zoo, or science organization is not beyond the realm of possibility. This can benefit both partners in a variety of ways, depending upon their needs. Your class can help field test curriculum or programs designed for elementary students being developed by a science museum or zoo. They may also enlist your help in writing this curriculum. Even though this is usually a volunteer task, you benefit from having your skills recognized, and the museum or

Consider having guest speakers visit your class to highlight different science careers.

zoo will have a much stronger curriculum thanks to your input. A partnership with a local high school science department can benefit your class if you are able to borrow equipment and perhaps have some of the students or teachers visit your class and do a hands-on science lesson. The high school students and teachers will discover how challenging this is and grow from the experience.

Partnerships can be as formal or informal as the parties involved agree upon. It is not necessary to have a partner who will offer financial assistance. The exchange of services can be extremely worthwhile to everyone in the partnership.

The suggestions described in this chapter will enhance your students' appreciation for science, as well as provide incentives to make it a vital part of their lives.

The next chapter will introduce Science Discovery Day, an exciting alternative to the science fair. Parent involvement will be an important component in presenting this event.

Science Discovery Day

Should I conduct a Science Discovery Day?

Science fairs in the elementary school are frequently a static display of projects which follow the scientific method and are often products of the efforts of parents and older brothers or sisters, rather than the elementary student. As mentioned in the "Overview" chapter of this book, the scientific method is not an appropriate technique to use when teaching science to elementary students. Science Discovery Day is an exciting new alternative to the typical science fair. It is an event which is much more related to a hands-on science program.

Science Discovery Day offers a wide variety of activity sessions for students to attend, much like attending a science conference. Presenters for these activities may be the teachers, parents, guests from local museums, colleges, hospitals, the zoo, and even some of the upper grade students. It is best to devote an entire day to this event since students will be attending three of four sessions. Presenters will repeat their activities three or four times, depending upon the number of sessions scheduled during the day. Schedule

> **Science Discovery Day is an exciting new alternative to the typical science fair.**

the sessions for 40–45 minutes with a 10 minute passing period between. This will enable the presenters to have time to involve students in an exciting science activity, then cleanup and prepare for the next group. A recess break for students and presenters midway through the event is a good idea.

The activities should be assigned to different grade levels, according to the nature of the activities and the choices of the presenters. There will need to be enough activities to spread the students into groups of 15–20 to make it easier for the presenter and to use less material per session. The whole school may be required to accommodate this event, including every classroom, the cafeteria, library, stage, and outside areas such as the playground and perhaps an adjoining park. Schedule Science Discovery Day during the season of the year which is most likely to provide good weather. If the date is near the end of the year, it may be the grande finale for all the super science programs which the students have experienced since the beginning of school.

Science Discovery Day is a schoolwide effort and needs coordination and long range planning to make it a success. Begin this planning at least three months before the date of the event. This date should be determined by the teachers, since they will play the most important roles. One or two people should be selected as coordinator(s). It is best to designate a teacher or administrator from the school for the position(s). A committee should be formed including teachers, parents, and possibly upper grade students. This committee is responsible for the following tasks:

◆ Determine the number of sessions.

◆ Solicit, select, and assign presenters and presiders.

◆ Organize a system for assigning students to the activities.

◆ Gather and purchase materials as needed.

◆ Announce the event and invite visitors.

◆ Arrange for a photographer.

◆ Arrange for greeters and tour guides for visitors.

◆ Troubleshoot and assist as needed at the event.

◆ Show appreciation for the presenters' efforts.

◆ Evaluate Science Discovery Day.

Subcommittees may be formed so teams can carry out the different responsibilities. Some require more time than others. The job of the coordinator includes convening and conducting committee meetings

> Science Discovery Day is a schoolwide effort and needs coordination and long range planning to make it a success.

and assuring that the tasks are being accomplished on time. The coordinator(s) should not conduct an activity for Science Discovery Day since they will be needed to act as troubleshooters throughout the sessions.

The first task of the committee is to develop a time line, starting backwards from the date for the Science Discovery Day. This time line should include the responsibilities shown above. Invite guest presenters as early as possible to be sure to get on their schedules. Before the first meeting ends, assign one or two people to assume responsibility for each of the tasks. They should be encouraged to find additional people to help them, so that no one is overburdened.

Distribute a call for volunteers to all parents and selected community members. Volunteers will be needed to serve as presenters, presiders, chaperones to help primary and special education students get to their sessions, and greeters and guides for visitors. Presiders will assist the presenters in putting out materials and cleaning up between sessions. They will also check at the beginning of each session to be sure the students are in the right place. During the activity they will assist the presenter as requested. Some additional volunteers will be needed to escort groups of kindergartners or special education students to their activities.

Distribute a call for volunteers to all parents and selected community members.

The Sample Volunteer Form on page 62 should be distributed to all parents. They can indicate whether they want to be presenters or presiders during Science Discovery Day. If they choose to be presenters, send them copies of the Presenter's Form on page 63.

Upper grade students may also be included as presenters. It is best to develop teams of six to do the activity so they can rotate through the three sessions in pairs, making it possible for them attend two other activities. The students will need training and an opportunity to practice presenting their activity. An adult presider should be assigned to remain with the student-led activity throughout all three sessions. Be sure to explain to the presiders that they will assist but not take over the instruction. The students will be responsible for conducting the activity. Students may also be assigned as presiders to help a presenter, perhaps working with their teacher.

The number of presenters needed will depend upon the student population. If the goal is to have 15 to 20 students in a group and there are about 600 students, plan on having at least 40 activities/presenters. All presenters, including teachers, should write descriptions of their activities, listing the materials they will need help in getting or will need to purchase. Expenses should be kept to a minimum by using inexpensive or donated items. Funds for reimbursing purchases may be available through the school's PTA or other parent group.

When selecting the activities, be sure they will actively involve the students rather than be a lecture or static display. Some examples are:

◆ Viewing a mineral collection will not involve the students as much as showing the minerals and then leading them through an activity to help them learn how to identify minerals.

◆ Watching a video on protecting wildlife can be extended into an activity by showing actual wild animals which have been rescued. Contact the local humane society to request a speaker for this topic.

◆ A demonstration of juggling will be far more exciting when students become actively involved by trying it for themselves, perhaps by using tennis balls.

When selecting the activities, be sure they will actively involve the students rather than be a lecture or static display.

If someone proposes an activity which does not involve the students, the coordinators may need to show how it can involve the students. This usually takes a bit of diplomacy but the presenter will benefit by discovering that teaching science requires skill in creating lessons that have students learn through participation.

Activities will need to be spread throughout the school. Most of the teachers will want to use their own classrooms. Some may be willing to do their activities outside and let guest presenters use their rooms. The cafeteria may handle several different activities. A stage can be used for an activity which requires a dark area. Outside activities may be found in the teachers' guides from *Project WILD: Elementary Activity Guide* (California Department of Fish and Game Conservation, 1986). If there is a stream or pond near the school, activities from *Project Wild Aquatic: Elementary Activity Guide* (1987) would be appropriate. Ideally, activities presented by the teachers should be extenders from science programs they conducted throughout the year. Additional ideas for science activities are available in many of the guides and references for teachers and activity science books listed in the "Resources" section.

Create a map of the school grounds and show the location of the activities and schedule for the sessions. Give maps to all presenters and make extra copies for the office staff and visitors. An example of such a map is shown at the end of this chapter on page 64. The titles of activities shown on the map will provide you with further ideas for topics which may be used for Science Discovery Day.

Assigning students to the different activities can be complicated, so using tickets for each activity will simplify this process. This ticket may look like the following example:

Sample Science Discovery Day Ticket

3	**Activity:** Snails **Grade** K–1 **Location:** Kindergarten Classroom **Presenter:** Mrs. Smith

The information shown on the ticket includes the activity number, title, grade range, location, and presenter. Each activity should have its own number to distinguish it from the others. One way to assign the ticket numbers is by grouping the activity titles according to grade levels. Print three copies of all tickets, one for each session. Color code the tickets for each session using three different colors such as green for session one, yellow for session two, and red for the last session.

Assigning students to the different activities can be complicated, so using tickets for each activity will simplify this process.

Distribute only the number of tickets which will be assigned to each activity, usually between 15 and 20. Determine the total number of students in each grade, create a list of the names of the activities by grade level, and assign the number of students. Keep the same number of students for each activity in all three sessions to make it easier for ticket distribution. An example of the list is shown below:

Tickets Per Session

# Topic	Gr.	K	1	2	3	4	5	6	Total
1 Discovery	K–1	7	8	x	x	x	x	x	15
2 Boats	K–1	7	8	x	x	x	x	x	15
3 Snails	K–1	7	8	x	x	x	x	x	15
4 Flubber	K–2	7	7	6	x	x	x	x	20

Be sure the total number of tickets distributed matches the number of students in each grade. The bottom of the list of activities and number of tickets would show these totals:

Totals
K=63 1=82 2=89 3=93 4=87 5=96 6=105 614

Once the number of tickets for each activity has been determined, assign them to the teachers in the school according to the grade level and number of students in each classroom. A random distribution of the tickets will ensure that a wide range of activities is available to the students in each classroom. At the end of the day, students can return to their classrooms and share their experiences, perhaps even showing something they made in their sessions. This is a great language arts extender for Science Discovery Day.

Do not overlook the need to advertise your special Science Discovery Day. Design an announcement to be sent home to all the families and distributed to school administrators and others who should be invited as special guests. Include information about the time schedule and list some of the titles of the activities. Invite other schools to send one or more representatives to observe the event. After they experience the excitement generated by Science Discovery Day, they may decide to borrow the idea for their schools.

Do not overlook the need to advertise your special Science Discovery Day.

Arrange for greeters to be at the school's entrance to offer maps to the visitors and conduct tours. This is a good role for the principal and PTA officers, since they are likely to know many of the visitors.

Have someone photograph the various activities, preferably using a video camera to record the students in action. The completed video can be rotated among the classrooms so students can relive the excitement of that day and see events which they were not able to attend. The videotape may also be used to provide other schools with an overview of the activities and assist them in creating ideas for their own Science Discovery Day.

If your school usually has several lunch sessions, it may be necessary to change the schedule on Science Discovery Day to permit enough time for all the activities. If you decide to have all students eat at the same time, invite them to bring sack lunches. Students can be assigned to eat in designated areas with adult supervisors.

It is important to show appreciation for the hard work done by the presenters and presiders. This may be done in the form of a potluck lunch provided by the school staff for the volunteers on the day of the event. Students can make thank you cards for the people involved in conducting Science Discovery Day so they can have the chance to express their appreciation and exhibit good manners. The children should be asked what they liked best about the day and what changes they suggest for next time the event is presented. This will assist in the evaluation of Science Discovery Day and provide ideas for the next year.

Although Science Discovery Day requires time and effort, the benefits are valuable science experiences for all the students at the school.

The next and last chapter, "Grande Finale," describes some alternatives for continuing and expanding students' enthusiasm for science after the regular school year ends. These include a special science summer school and using a college campus for upper elementary and middle school students to attend unique science classes.

(Sample Volunteer Form)

Orion School
Announces a Special Event:
Science Discovery Day
Thursday, May 25, 1995
9:00 – 11:35 A.M.

Call for Volunteers

Science Discovery Day is a day filled with science activities for all the students at the school. There will be three 40 minute sessions during the morning. Approximately 40 activities will be presented during each of the sessions. The schedule will be:

9:00 – 9:40   Session 1
9:50 – 10:30   Session 2 (same activities, different students)
10:30 – 10:50 Recess break
10:55 – 11:35 Session 3 (final session)

We need your help to make our Science Discovery Day a success. If you are interested in participating as a volunteer presenter to do an activity, a presider to help someone who is a presenter, or offer other assistance, please complete the form below. If you have any questions, please call the school.

Science Discovery Day
Volunteer Form

Please return this form to school by Friday, March 17, 1994.
Please print the following information:
Name: _____ Phone: _____
_____ I would like to assist as a presider from 8:45 – 11:35 A.M.
_____ I would like to assist as needed from 8:45 – 11:35 A.M.
_____ I would like to present a science activity. (You will be sent a presenter's form to give more information about your activity.)

Orion School
Science Discovery Day
Thursday, May 25, 1995
9:00 – 11:35 A.M.

Call for Presenters

Science Discovery Day is a day filled with science activities for all the students at the school. There will be three 40 minute sessions during the morning. The schedule will be:

     9:00 – 9:40   Session 1
     9:50 – 10:30   Session 2 (same activities, different students)
     10:30 – 10:50 Recess break
     10:55 – 11:35 Session 3 (final session)

Approximately 40 activities are needed for Science Discovery Day. The same activities will be repeated during each of the three sessions. If you would like to be a presenter of an activity, complete the form below. If you have any questions, please call the school.

Science Discovery Day
Presenter Form

Please return this form to school by Monday, April 10, 1995.

Name: _____ Position: _____

Home Phone: _____ Work Phone: _____

Home or work address: _____

Activity Topic: _____

Appropriate for grades (circle): K–2 3–4 5–6 K–6

Area best suited for this activity (circle): classroom, playground, patio, cafeteria, library, park

Attach a brief description of your activity. Include a list of materials you may need to purchase or borrow to do this activity. You will have about 20 students assigned to each of the three sessions. Save the receipts for any purchases you make and submit them for reimbursement after Science Discovery Day.

Science Discovery Day Map
Orion School

Kites and Juggling
(Lower Playground)

Discovery Walk
(Park)

Room 22 Lemons to Lemonade	Room 21 Optricks	Room 20 Signal Flags	Room 19 Owl Pellets	Room 18 Pets	Restrooms

Bubbles
(Sandbox Area)

Room 17 Gliders	Room 16 Airplanes	Room 15 Go for Launch	Room 14 Electric Circuits	Room 13 Colored Solutions

Restrooms	Room 12 Finger Paints	Room 11 Bridges	Room 10 Chemical Magic	Room 9 Structures

Geology
(Patio)

Room 8 Crystal Gardens	Room 7 Magnets	Room 6 Show & Tell	Room 5 Sorting	Room 4 Flubber

Office
Lounge
K Classroom
Good Vibrations

Parachutes
(Upper Playground)

Room 3 Fish Dissection	Room 2 Mealworms	Room 1 Dry Ice Fossils

Schedule:
Session 1— 9:00 - 9:40
Session 2—9:50 - 10:30
Recess—10:30 - 10:50
Session 3—10:55 - 11:35
Lunch—11:45

Grande Finale

How can science continue after school ends?

If your school offers summer programs, consider designing the classes around science themes for each grade level. Teachers will have the opportunity to develop and test new science programs which they can then apply to students in their regular classrooms. It may even be possible to have students from other schools in the district attend this special Science Summer School.

Science Summer School

Initiate the concept of a Science Summer School early in the school year to permit time for organizing it. Begin by discussing this idea with your school administrator and fellow teachers, and perhaps even expand it to include administrators in the school district to form an action group. You may be pleasantly surprised at the support you receive from parents and teachers who realize that a Science Summer School will be very beneficial to elementary students. Concentrating on a variety of science topics at different grade levels in the summer can provide stimulating experiences for the students. There may be greater opportunities to explore science

> Initiate the concept of a Science Summer School early in the school year to permit time for organizing it.

beyond the school site during the summer programs, since these programs tend to be less formal than those during the regular school year. Plan to include science study trips and guest speakers in the summer program to enrich the topics being covered.

Encourage the involvement of teachers who have a sincere interest in improving their science programs by requiring applicants to submit a science course proposal. The proposal should outline a hands-on curriculum which covers a specific science theme or topic. Include a balance of classes offering other subjects which will support the science topics, such as mathematics, fine arts, literature, and social studies. Teachers can team up in order to offer the special lessons they have developed to more than one group of students by rotating them throughout the day. Classes can be scheduled so that students can take three or more during the day, permitting a combination of science and other subjects that relate to and enrich the science programs.

College for Kids

College for Kids can be conducted on a college, university, or community college campus to have access to unique facilities such as science labs and perhaps even a planetarium. There may also be the possibility of involving college faculty to teach some of the classes. Just be sure they embrace the technique of teaching science through hands-on experiences rather than lecturing to the students.

A College for Kids summer program for gifted and high achieving students entering fifth through ninth grades has been conducted at Southwestern College in Chula Vista, California, since 1974. Staff members are drawn from this community college, local schools, and specialists such as artists and gymnasts. A teaching credential is not required, but teaching experience is necessary. Teachers for this program are chosen by the College for Kids Board which consists of representatives from the college and the six local school districts, who are frequently the coordinators of programs for gifted students. Staff selection is done on the basis of course proposals with the criteria for acceptance those which offer unique challenges and a balance of subject areas. The classes are conducted Monday through Thursday from 1:00 to 4:00 P.M.

This three week program, begins in late June and runs until mid-July, between the end of the 10 month school year and before the year-round schools open. A fee is charged for two, two hour classes which meet for 12 days. Course offerings have included a variety of science classes conducted in biology and chemistry laboratories, as well as the planetarium. Other subjects such as physical education, literature,

> **Encourage the involvement of teachers who have a sincere interest in improving their science programs by requiring applicants to submit a science course proposal.**

66

computers, mathematics, and a variety of fine arts are also offered. Some classes, such as the art classes, require an additional fee for materials.

The program is self supporting through the fees which are charged. Scholarships which pay 50% of the fee are available to those who can prove financial need. By paying only half the fees, scholarship funds can be extended to more students. One of the participating school districts with a high percentage of families at or below the poverty level raised funds for scholarships to enable their students to attend. The registration form invites parents to make a tax deductible contribution to the scholarship fund and donations are solicited by the College for Kids board members. Southwestern College Foundation also makes an annual contribution to the scholarship fund.

How can I improve my science background?

The mere fact that you are reading this book, and particularly this section, most likely indicates you are interested in developing an area of expertise in elementary science. One of the best ways to begin to improve your science background is to attend local, state, and national science conferences. There you will be able to attend a variety of science sessions, usually presented by teachers who have designed their own science activities. This will provide you with a wide range of science ideas and materials to use with your students. It will also provide you the opportunity to get to meet the presenters and perhaps get individual help in designing your own lessons and units. Do not overlook the chance to attend sessions provided for middle and high school teachers or the general sessions presented by prominent scientists. These will add to your science knowledge and may encourage you to continue your own education in science.

One of the best ways to begin to improve your science background is to attend local, state, and national science conferences.

Check the catalogs of your local community colleges and investigate extension courses offered by the colleges and universities near you to find science classes in which you can enroll and even earn college credit. These are frequently designed for participants who do not have much of a science background. Education is a lifelong pursuit and is often more meaningful when you are an adult. This may be especially true for teachers.

Search bookstores for books which will develop your science background; many of these are listed in the "Resources" section of this book. They can provide science information which is easy to understand without having college courses or a degree in science. These books will serve as great references as you design your lessons and units. They can also be useful to your students who are as fascinated by science as you are. Consider developing a library of science books for your use as well as to loan to trustworthy students and fellow teachers.

High school science teachers are often willing to be mentors for elementary teachers. They have the experience working with students who do not have much science background. Do not let pride get in your way; ask questions which will help you learn what you want to know. Just because you are an adult and a teacher does not mean you are expected to know everything. We often develop more empathy for our students when we become students ourselves.

High school science teachers are often willing to be mentors for elementary teachers.

Teacher workshops are frequently presented by school districts or federally and state funded projects. Information about these workshops can be obtained through reading *Science and Children*, the National Science Teachers Association (NSTA) journal for elementary teachers. Check the "Resources" section for the address of NSTA. Membership in this national association, and your local and state science teachers organizations, is another way of expanding your science background through the journals and newsletters provided the members, as well as getting information about conferences they sponsor.

Teacher Created Materials offers teacher workshops across the nation on many of their teacher guides, including the science series. For a schedule of workshops, call (800) 662-4321.

Hopefully, the information shared with the reader in this book will be useful and inspire the development of programs for elementary students that result in an appreciation and excitement for all the areas of science. It is only through the enthusiastic teacher that students will become aware of the true value of the study of science.

References

American Association for the Advancement of Science. (1990). Project 2061: Science for all Americans. New York: Oxford University Press. [A set of recommendations on what understandings and ways of thinking are essential for all citizens in a world shaped by science.]

Barry, D. (1994). Easy chemistry: Intermediate. Westminster, CA: Teacher Created Materials. [A hands-on teacher's guide covering topics on matter, chemical properties and reactions, as well as the natural locations of chemicals.]

California Department of Fish and Game Conservation. (1986). Project WILD: Elementary activity guide. Sacramento, CA: Author. [This teacher's guide contains 81 lessons that investigate the biology, behavior, and ecology of animals.]

California State Department of Education. (1990). Science framework for California public schools. Sacramento, CA: Author. [Contains chapters on the nature of science, major themes of science, science content, achieving desired science curriculum, and suggestions for science programs and content matrix for K–12.]

Cannon, J. (1993). Stellaluna. San Diego, CA: Harcourt. [This beautifully illustrated book tells the humorous story of a young bat, Stellaluna, separated from her mother before she is young enough to fly and raised in the bird nest into which she falls. She adapts to the habits of her new family, the birds, until she rediscovers her own kind.]

Cole, J. C. (1994). The magic school bus in the time of the dinosaurs. New York: Scholastic. [One of a series of science books which delightfully mixes fact and fantasy.]

Horner, J., & Gorman, J. (1989). Maia, a dinosaur grows up. Philadelphia, PA: Running Press. [A realistic fictional account of the life of a young Maiasaura dinosaur based upon the research of Dr. John Horner, a paleontologist. Through the eyes of Maia, we learn of the everyday events and the perils of growing up in the world of dinosaurs, from hatching to maturity.]

Jasmine, J. (1994). Science assessment: Grades 3–4. Westminster, CA: Teacher Created Materials. [This teacher's guide includes the topics of portfolios, anecdotal records, and a variety of other alternative assessment techniques, as well as end of the third and fourth grade science curricular expectations.]

McNulty, F. (1979). How to dig a hole to the other side of the world. New York: Harper Collins Publishers. [A charming story about how to dig to the other side of the earth, this book contains colorful illustrations and correct scientific information. It is appropriate for primary and middle elementary grades.]

Project WILD. (1987). Project WILD aquatic: Education activity guide. Boulder, CO: Author. [This guide consists of 40 activities that explore the world of water.]

Schatz, D. (1987). Dinosaurs: A journey through time. Seattle, WA: Pacific Science Center. [An activity-oriented resource book for teachers and elementary students presenting updated information about dinosaurs.]

References *(cont.)*

Wildlife Education. <u>Zoobooks</u>. San Diego, CA: Author. [A monthly publication, each on a different topic such as Owls, Whales, and Dinosaurs. Colorful pictures and diagrams make these periodicals a valuable reference source. Back issues may be ordered or purchased at many science museum shops.]

Young, R. (1994). <u>Geology: Intermediate</u>. Westminster, CA: Teacher Created Materials. [A complete set of hands-on science lessons covering Earth's geologic time line, plate tectonics, and the causes and locations of earthquakes.]

Young, R. (1994). <u>Rocks and minerals: Primary</u>. Westminster, CA: Teacher Created Materials. [A teacher guide which provides activity lessons on the rock cycle, identification of minerals, and growing crystals.]

Young, R. (1994). <u>Space: Intermediate</u>. Westminster, CA: Teacher Created Materials. [This teacher's guide gives hands-on lessons on topics including the solar system, history of space exploration, and the moon and sun.]

Resources

Science Series

Delta Science Modules. Delta Education, Inc., P. O. Box 915, Hudson, NH 03051-0915. (800) 258-1302. [This series consists of teacher guides of 40 science subjects, as well as kits of equipment which can be purchased separately. Manuals are available for topics in the life, earth, and physical sciences. Each contains student activities and science background for the teacher.]

Full Option Science System (FOSS). Encyclopedia Britannica Educational Corp., 310 South Michigan Ave., 6th Floor, Chicago, IL 60604-9839. (800) 554-9862. [Each of these 27 modules has an extensive teacher guide in a loose leaf notebook which provides complete information for conducting activities on that particular topic. FOSS kits which contain all materials needed to conduct the lessons can also be purchased.]

Great Exploration in Math and Science (GEMS). Lawrence Hall of Science, University of California, Berkeley, CA 94720. (415) 642-7771. [More than 40 teacher guides for science and math activities using a guided discovery approach with topics such as acid rain, bubbleology, and earth, moon, and stars.]

Hands-On Minds-On Science. Teacher Created Materials, 6421 Industry Way, Westminster, CA 92683. (800) 662-4321. [Covers a wide variety of topics in earth, life, and physical sciences for students from early childhood to upper elementary. Each guide is a science unit consisting of activities, curriculum connections, assessment, glossary, and list of resources.]

Science and Technology for Children. Carolina Biological Supply Co., 2700 York Road, Burlington, NC 27215. (800) 334-5551. [The National Science Resources Center has designed 24 hands-on science units for grades 1–6 consisting of lessons for eight weeks of instruction.]

Science Materials by Mail Order

Astronomical Society of the Pacific, 390 Ashton Ave., San Francisco, CA 94112. [Supplies astronomy slides, videotapes, posters, books, and other items.]

California Division of Mines and Geology, Publication Sales, P. O. Box 2980, Sacramento, CA 95812. [Request a catalog which lists maps regarding earthquakes in California.]

Carolina Biological Supply Co., 2700 York Rd., Burlington, NC 27215. [Supplies a wealth of life science materials; request a free catalog.]

Cynmar Scientific Co., P. O. Box 530, Carlinville, IL 62626. [Discount supplier of science equipment, including microscopes and microprojector.]

Dale Seymour Publications, P. O. Box 10888, Palo Alto, CA 94303-0879. [Supplier of teacher's manuals, reference and trade books, posters, and videos in the area of science as well as other subjects.]

Delta Education, Inc., P. O. Box 915, Hudson, NH 03051-0915. [Request a catalog of materials for Elementary Science Study (ESS), Outdoor Biology Instructional Strategies (OBIS), Science: A Process Approach (SAPA), and Science Curriculum Improvement Study (SCIIS3).]

Edmund Scientific, 101 E. Gloucester Pike, Barrington, NJ 08007-1380. [Suppliers of science materials which are often difficult to find.]

Resources *(cont.)*

Science Materials by Mail Order *(cont.)*

Insect Lore, P. O. Box 1535, Shafter, CA 93263. [A large selection of science materials, including live butterfly larva, silkworms, earthworms, and praying mantis egg cases. Other items include owl pellets and books for students and teachers.]

National Geographic Society, P. O. Box 2118, Washington, DC 20013-2118. [Request copies of the member catalog as well as one of maps, globes, and atlases. Materials include science books, videotapes, maps, and posters.]

National Science Teachers Association (NSTA), 1840 Wilson Blvd., Arlington, VA 22201-3000. [Request a copy of NSTA science education suppliers, an annual publication listing equipment suppliers, educational services, computer software, media producers, and publishers of science materials. Request a free catalog listing other NSTA publications.]

Ward's Natural Science Establishment, 5100 West Henrietta Rd., Rochester, NY 14692. [Suppliers of mineral specimens and many other science materials.]

Guides and Reference Books for the Teacher

Audubon Society Pocket Guides. New York: Chanticleer Press. [This pocket sized series on various topics such as birds and insects contains beautiful detailed photographs of individual specimens. Brief information is given about each of the animals illustrated. Look for these books in science shops and bookstores.]

Bosak, S. (1991). Science is.....A sourcebook of fascinating facts, projects and activities. Richmond Hill, Ontario: Scholastic Canada LTD. [This book is packed with great science activities on a wide range of topics.]

Gega, P. C. (1994). Concepts and experiences in elementary school science. New York: Macmillan Publishing Co. [A teacher's guide which provides background and related activities on a wide range of science topics.]

Gega, P. C. (1994). How to teach elementary school science. New York: Macmillan Publishing Co. [This books covers philosophy of teaching science as well as practical ideas.]

Golden Guide Series. New York: Golden Press. [This series of pocket sized books is an easy reference guide to a wide variety of science topics such as planets, rocks and minerals, and birds. Look for this series in science stores and bookstores.]

Imes, R. (1992). The practical entomologist. New York: Simon & Schuster/Fireside. [A beautifully illustrated introduction to insects that takes an order-by-order look, explaining how each group differs from another. Activities to study insects are interspersed with careful descriptions of appearance and habitat. Appropriate for upper elementary students and as a teacher reference book.]

Instant guide to... Series. Stanford, CT: Longmeadow Press. [These handy pocket sized guides cover a variety of science topics including: reptiles and amphibians, stars and planets, and rocks and minerals. The colorful illustrations and easy to follow descriptions make the books great references for elementary students and teachers. These books are found in science stores and bookstores.]

Resources *(cont.)*

Guides and Reference Books for the Teacher *(cont.)*

Lambert, D. (1988). The field guide to geology. New York: Facts on File. [An easy-to-use reference guide for upper elementary students and their teachers. This book provides concise information on the key ingredients and processes that forged our planet. Hundreds of clearly labeled diagrams and illustrations are interwoven with text written for a beginner in geology. Other field guides by the same author include The field guide to prehistoric life (1988) and The field guide to early man (1987).]

Stein, S. (1986). The evolution book. New York: Workman Publishing. [Travel in time beginning 4,000 million years ago through the great ice age as you read this book. Information and activities scattered throughout the text make this a wonderful resource for teaching evolution to upper elementary and middle school students.]

The visual dictionary of the universe. (1993). New York: Dorling Kindersley. [Part of a series, this book provides a wide range of topics on astronomy from planets to the universe. It is a colorfully illustrated reference appropriate for teachers and upper grade students.]

Activity Science and Science Literature for Elementary Students

Cobb, V. (1985). Chemically alive: Experiments you can do at home. New York: J. B. Lippincott. [This book contains easy to do activities in chemistry. It is one of a series written by Vicki Cobb which provides great science activities that are fun and easy to do and use inexpensive materials.]

Dickson, T. (1987). Exploring the night sky. Camden East, Ontario: Camden House Publishing. [A guide to the stars aimed at novice stargazers anxious to expand their astronomical knowledge beyond the Big Dipper. Ideal for upper elementary students and as a reference for teachers.]

Dimensional Nature Portfolio Series. (1991). New York: Workman Publishing. [The ultimate series in pop-up books covering topics including bees, spiders, and butterflies. The center of each book has a large, detailed pop-up of the subject. The text gives brief, interesting information and mini-pop-ups of body parts and habitats.]

Macaulay, D. (1988). The way things work. Boston, MA: Houghton Mifflin. [This amusing book not only illustrates and explains how machines do what they do, but also shows how the concept behind one invention is linked to the concept of another invention.]

Mammana, D. (1989). The night sky. Philadelphia, PA: Running Press. [A "user friendly" astronomy book suggests a variety of activities to teach about the sun, moon, planets, and stars. It is appropriate for grades 3–6.]

Van Cleave, J. (1991). Earth science for every kid. New York: John Wiley & Sons, Inc. [Like Vicki Cobb, this author has written a series of hands-on science guides which are filled with easy and fun to do science activities. Others in this series cover topics of biology, chemistry, astronomy, and physics.]

Resources *(cont.)*

Science Periodicals for Elementary Students

3-2-1 Contact. Children's Television Workshop, One Lincoln Plaza, New York, NY 10023.
[This magazine contains puzzles, projects, experiments and interesting science events around
the world.]

Odyssey. Cobblestone Publishing, 7 School Street, Peterborough, NH 03458-1454. [Devoted
to space exploration and astronomy topics.]

Ranger Rick. National Wildlife Federation, 1412 16th Street NW, Washington, DC 20036-2266.
[The goal of this magazine is to help children learn to enjoy nature and appreciate the need
for conservation by providing motivating activities.]

SuperScience. Scholastic, 555 Broadway, New York, NY, 10012-3999. [This periodical comes
in two editions: Red for grades 1–3 and Blue for grades 4–6. It covers a variety of topics and
activities in science.]

Science Associations and Organizations

There are local, state, and national science organizations that offer assistance to their members
through newsletters, journals, conferences, and reviews of science materials. Although this list is
not complete, it will offer the reader a wide range of national science organizations from which to
choose. Additional information regarding your state and local organizations can be obtained by
contacting your science representatives at the school district or state level. Membership in your
local science organization can often lead to networking that will provide you with the ideas and
guidance you need to develop your science program.

Astronomical Society of the Pacific (ASP), 390 Ashton Ave., San Francisco, CA 94112.
[Newsletter for teachers and activities for students and teachers.]

Educational Products Information Exchange (EPIE), P. O. Box 839, Water Mill, NY 11976
[Publishes *The Educational Software Selection* (TESS) and newsletters (*EPIEGRAM* and
MICROGRAM) and sponsors the CASE program involved with curriculum alignment in
schools nationwide.]

Educational Resources Information Center (ERIC), Ohio State University, 1200 Chambers Road,
Third Floor, Columbus, OH 43212. [Clearinghouse for published and unpublished materials
relating to science, mathematics, and environmental education. The Elementary Science
Study (ESS) and Unified Science and Mathematics for Elementary Schools (USMES)
curriculum materials are accessible on-line or supplied on microfiche or photocopy for a fee.]

National Aeronautics and Space Administration (NASA), NASA Headquarters, Code XEE,
Washington, DC 20546. [Provides specialists for school visits and educational materials for
teachers through the CORE project. Also disseminates materials at each of the nine NASA
centers and more than 20 regional centers. Write to request the NASA center closest to
you.]

National Audubon Society, 613 Riversville Road, Greenwich, CT 06830. [Publishes a nature
newspaper for children, *Audubon Adventures*, produces software and television specials and
conducts workshops and a summer ecology camp for teachers.]

Resources *(cont.)*

Science Associations and Organizations *(cont.)*

National Science Resource Center (NSRC), Smithsonian Institution, Washington, DC 20560.
[The mission of NSRC is to contribute to the improvement of science and mathematics
teaching in the nation's schools by establishing a science and mathematics curriculum resource
center and information database, developing and disseminating resource materials for science
and mathematics teachers, and offering a program of outreach and leadership development
activities.]

National Science Teachers Association (NSTA), 1840 Wilson Blvd., Arlington, VA 22201-3000.
[Numerous professional publications, newsletters, and resource materials for science teachers,
including *Science and Children*, a membership magazine for elementary school teachers.
This magazine highlights science suppliers in its January issue and science trade books for
children in the March issue. The magazine also contains a wealth of curriculum ideas written
by teachers from across the nation. Write to NSTA to request information regarding
your state science teachers association.]

National Wildlife Federation, 1400 16th Street NW, Washington, DC 20036. [Publishes science
magazines and curriculum materials including the *Ranger Rick* magazine and *NatureScope*
series of activity guides for teachers.]

Smithsonian Institution, Education Dept., Arts and Industries Bldg., Room 1163, Washington,
DC 20560. [Sponsors teacher-training programs and special events and produces *ART-TO-
ZOO*, a free newsletter for teachers.]

Resources *(cont.)*

Teacher Created Materials Reference List

Hands-On Minds-On Science

Each book contains hands-on activities, teacher information about science process skills, unit organization, and curriculum connections.

Earth Science:
TCM #633 Ecology (Primary)
TCM #634 Space (Primary
TCM #636 Rocks and Minerals (Primary)
TCM #638 Environmental Issues (Intermediate)
TCM #639 Space (Intermediate)
TCM #641 Geology (Intermediate)

Life Science:
TCM #625 Plants (Primary)
TCM #626 Animals (Primary)
TCM #628 Endangered Species (Primary)
TCM #629 Plants (Intermediate)
TCM #630 Animals (Intermediate)
TCM #632 Endangered Species (Intermediate)

Physical Science:
TCM #643 Magnetism & Electricity
   (Primary)
TCM #644 Simple Machines (Primary)
TCM #645 Simple Chemistry (Primary)
TCM #646 Magnetism & Electricity
   (Intermediate)
TCM #647 Force & Motion (Intermediate)
TCM #648 Easy Chemistry (Intermediate)

Assessment Series

This series of books is designed to help educators adopt new assessment strategies.

TCM #771 Science Assessment, Grades 1–2
TCM #775 Science Assessment, Grades 3–4
TCM #779 Science Assessment, Grades 5–6

Other Science Resources

TCM #197 Science in a Bag (Primary)
Intriquing activities that students may share with their families.

TCM #341 Connecting Science and Literature (Primary)
Literature and supporting activities for all areas of science.

TCM #493 Focus on Scientists, Grades 4–8
Biographies, portraits, and activities for 30 scientists.